NEW DIRECTIONS FOR PROGRAM EVALUATION
A Publication of the American Evaluation Association

William R. Shadish, *Memphis State University*
EDITOR-IN-CHIEF

The Preparation of Professional Evaluators: Issues, Perspectives, and Programs

James W. Altschuld
The Ohio State University

Molly Engle
University of Alabama at Birmingham

EDITORS

Number 62, Summer 1994

JOSSEY-BASS PUBLISHERS
San Francisco

THE PREPARATION OF PROFESSIONAL EVALUATORS: ISSUES, PERSPECTIVES, AND PROGRAMS
James W. Altschuld, Molly Engle (eds.)
New Directions for Program Evaluation, no. 62
William R. Shadish, Editor-in-Chief

Microfilm copies of issues and articles are available in 16mm and 35mm, as well as microfiche in 105mm, through University Microfilms Inc., 300 North Zeeb Road, Ann Arbor, Michigan 48106-1346.

LC 85-644749   ISSN 0164-7989   ISBN 0-7879-9968-7

NEW DIRECTIONS FOR PROGRAM EVALUATION is part of The Jossey-Bass Education Series and is published quarterly by Jossey-Bass Inc., Publishers, 350 Sansome Street, San Francisco, California 94104-1342.

Subscriptions for 1994 cost $54.00 for individuals and $75.00 for institutions, agencies, and libraries.

EDITORIAL CORRESPONDENCE should be sent to the Editor-in-Chief, William R. Shadish, Department of Psychology, Memphis State University, Memphis, Tennessee 38152.

Manufactured in the United States of America. Nearly all Jossey-Bass books, jackets, and periodicals are printed on recycled paper that contains at least 50 percent recycled waste, including 10 percent postconsumer waste. Many of our materials are also printed with vegetable-based inks; during the printing process, these inks emit fewer volatile organic compounds (VOCs) than petroleum-based inks. VOCs contribute to the formation of smog.

Editorial Policy and Procedures

New Directions for Program Evaluation (NDPE), a quarterly sourcebook, is an official publication of the American Evaluation Association. NDPE publishes empirical, methodological, and theoretical works on all aspects of evaluation and related fields. Substantive areas may include any program, field, or issue with which evaluation is concerned, such as government performance, tax policy, energy, environment, mental health, education, job training, medicine, and public health. Also included are such topics as product evaluation, personnel evaluation, policy analysis, and technology assessment. In all cases, the focus on evaluation is more important than the substantive topics. We are particularly interested in encouraging a diversity of evaluation perspectives and experiences and in expanding the boundaries of our field beyond the evaluation of social programs.

NDPE does not consider or publish unsolicited single manuscripts. Each issue of NDPE is devoted to a single topic, with contributions solicited, organized, reviewed, and edited by a guest editor. Issues may take any of several forms, such as a series of related chapters, a debate, or a long article followed by brief critical commentaries. In all cases, the proposals must follow a specific format, which can be obtained from the editor-in-chief. These proposals are sent to members of the editorial board and to relevant substantive experts for peer review. The process may result in acceptance, a recommendation to revise and resubmit, or rejection. However, NDPE is committed to working constructively with potential guest editors to help them develop acceptable proposals.

Lois-ellin Datta, Editor-in-Chief
P.O. Box 383768
Waikoloa, HI 96738

Jennifer C. Greene, Associate Editor
Department of Human Service Studies
Cornell University
Ithaca, NY 14853-4401

Gary Henry, Associate Editor
Public Administration and Urban Studies
Georgia State University
Atlanta, GA 30302-4039

CONTENTS

Editors' Notes

The preparation of professional evaluators is an ongoing process—one that engages many individuals in universities, colleges, and government agencies. The board of the American Evaluation Association (AEA) believes that this topic is pivotal to the growth and development both of the profession and of the association. Under the board's direction, we have undertaken the most recent effort to document existing preparation programs. However, the simple documenting of the existence of a preparation program is only one part of this important topic. Issues and concerns about preparation and about the status of existing programs must also be addressed, and they are the focus of this volume.

Reviewing current thinking on the preparation of future members of the evaluation profession allows its members to see progress, identify where growth can occur, and preserve its history. This process allows them to reflect on what the field of evaluation is and on what it could be. We think that the chapters in this sourcebook will enrich our understanding and clarify our deliberations about this most vital aspect of evaluation.

In Chapter One, Blaine Worthen analyzes evaluation as a profession that warrants specialized training. He identifies nine criteria for a profession and thoughtfully describes evaluation in relation to them. In Chapter Two, Donna Mertens divides the skills and knowledge necessary for professional practice into two categories: the skills and knowledge already taught in other areas and those taught specifically in evaluation. She also calls our attention to the need for sensitivity as evaluators work in and with diverse groups and complex societies. In Chapter Three, Arnold Love tackles the difficult question of certification for evaluators. His chapter examines various aspects of this particularly delicate issue.

The next three chapters consider the development of evaluation preparation programs. In Chapter Four, Jody Fitzpatrick suggests that we train evaluators primarily to be practitioners and that we would benefit by choosing educational models like the ones found in professional schools. In Chapter Five, Michael Morris discusses the value of the single evaluation courses that often are located in smaller institutions. He playfully depicts the importance of single-course programs in educating future consumers of evaluation reports as well as in educating participants in the evaluation process. Nancy Kingsbury and Terry Hedrick present an example of a very large program within a government agency in Chapter Six.

Chapter Seven—by James Altschuld, Molly Engle, Carol Cullen, Inyoung Kim, and Barbara Rae Macce—contains the 1994 directory of evaluation training programs, which is preceded by a brief description of the procedures used to produce it. The authors of Chapter Seven would like to thank the board of the American Evaluation Association; the AEA's past, current, and incoming presidents—David Cordray, David Fetterman, and Karen Kirkhart, respectively; Arnold Love, president of the Canadian Evaluation Society (CES); the regional CES presidents; Kathy Jones of the CES; Gary Cox of the University of Washington; the National Center for Science Teaching and Learning at The Ohio State University; HealthEast of St. Paul, Minnesota; and the University of Alabama School of Medicine for assistance with preparation of the directory. The editors of this volume express their deep gratitude to those who participated in the study. Without them, it would not have been possible.

James W. Altschuld
Molly Engle
Editors

JAMES W. ALTSCHULD is associate professor of educational research and evaluation and evaluation coordinator for the National Center for Science Teaching and Learning at The Ohio State University. His research interests include evaluation models and methodology, needs assessment, and the development of evaluation training programs.

MOLLY ENGLE is an assistant professor in the Behavioral Medicine Unit, Division of Preventive Medicine, Department of Medicine at the University of Alabama at Birmingham School of Medicine. She designs, implements, and conducts research and evaluations in behavioral medicine and community-based health services.

Criteria for judging the maturity of any profession are applied to evaluation. Special attention is paid to the question of whether programs for the preparation of evaluation specialists are warranted.

Is Evaluation a Mature Profession That Warrants the Preparation of Evaluation Professionals?

Blaine R. Worthen

There is wide agreement that evaluation is an important professional specialization, but there is less certainty as to whether it has yet attained the status of a distinct profession. To answer this question, I propose that a fully developed profession has at least nine characteristics, and I will discuss these characteristics in the context of the need for preparation. Worthen and Sanders (1991) advanced six of these criteria in their discussion of trends in educational evaluation, and portions of this chapter draw on that earlier work.

First, a fully developed profession needs persons with specialized knowledge and skills. Second, it has developed a body of content (knowledge and skills) unique to its area of specialization. Third, the profession has developed preparation programs designed to produce practitioners who are well qualified in the unique knowledge and skills. Fourth, stable career opportunities have emerged for such well-qualified practitioners. Fifth, the specialization has developed procedures for the certification or licensure of those judged qualified to practice it. Sixth, the specialization has developed associations devoted to furthering the professional development of its practitioners. Seventh, the specialization has developed criteria for determining membership in such associations. Eighth, the relevant professional associations influence the preparation programs. Ninth, the specialization has developed standards to guide those who practice it.

A simple status check on each of the nine criteria proposed would be one way of judging how far evaluation has moved toward attaining the characteristics of a full-fledged profession. However, the maturation of evaluation toward the status of a profession can better be understood by considering the forces that have shaped it across the past thirty years. Although space will not permit me to say much about the historical emergence and evolution of evaluation, I will sketch some portions of the historical backdrop when it helps me to clarify the current status of evaluation on the nine criteria proposed.

Need for Evaluation Specialists

Although there were a few embryonic efforts to evaluate public programs prior to 1960 (Shadish, Cook, and Leviton, 1991; Worthen and Sanders, 1987), most commentators believe that contemporary evaluation of educational and social programs first emerged during the 1960s. Early in that decade, the U.S. Congress passed federal legislation that, in authorizing antipoverty, juvenile delinquency prevention, and manpower development and training programs, both required program evaluation and allocated funds for it (Wholey, 1986; Weiss, 1987). Yet the emphasis on evaluation built into the Elementary and Secondary Education Act (ESEA) of 1965 dwarfed previous efforts to mandate the use of evaluation. Broad in scope, the ESEA provided large-scale funding for education that allowed tens of thousands of federal grants to be awarded to local schools, state and regional education agencies, and universities. Due largely to the efforts of Robert F. Kennedy, the ESEA required the recipients of grants dealing either with compensatory education for disadvantaged youth or with innovative educational projects (the great majority of grants) to file an evaluation report showing what had resulted from the expenditure of public funds.

Overnight, thousands of educators were required to evaluate their own efforts. Few were up to the task. Classroom teachers and building principals were among those pressed into technical activities for which they had little training. The results were abysmal. And when well-trained educational, psychological, or sociological researchers were called in to help, the results were—surprisingly—not much better. Despite their technical prowess, these researchers were not prepared for the complex tasks of identifying the influences that could be attributed to each of several components of a program or even of separating the effects of the program from other activities going on in the school. Clearly, new evaluation approaches, methods, and strategies were needed.

Meanwhile, areas outside education were experiencing increased demands for evaluation, although it was often called by other names. By the late 1960s, Congress had authorized monies for evaluation of social programs in areas as diverse as the Job Corps, vocational rehabilitation, child health, and community action. Managers of the projects and programs funded under such social legislation searched to find the individuals best equipped to fill the newly created evaluation roles. Faced with an absence of persons trained directly in evaluation, they employed people trained for roles that contained some evaluative functions—professional accountants and auditors; management consultants; planning and systems analysts; economists; research, product development, and test marketing specialists from the private sector; and academics in areas relevant to the collection and analysis of evaluative information (Shadish, Cook, and Leviton, 1991).

The evaluations conducted by these persons were little better than those conducted by the classroom teachers and educational psychologists who had been pressed into service as evaluators on federally funded education projects. While most of those drafted or recruited into evaluation roles were very skillful in some of the tasks required of evaluators, few were even aware of the broad range of tasks that were essential for a complete and adequate evaluation. Fewer still possessed the skills that one must have in order to complete those tasks. The need for persons with a new constellation of specialized skills was evident to any insightful observer.

Today the need for evaluation specialists is generally accepted, although many policy makers and program managers who are naive about the knowledge and skills that evaluators should possess still attribute evaluation expertise to self-appointed or self-anointed "evaluators" who lack essential evaluation skills and knowledge. Despite the frequent lapses when evaluators are selected, that there is a need for evaluation specialists seems to be well established.

Development of Unique Content

When demands for evaluation increased dramatically in the 1960s, the resulting evaluation studies revealed the conceptual and methodological impoverishment of evaluation as it then existed. Theoretical and methodological work related directly to evaluation did not exist, and evaluators were left to gather what they could from theories in cognate disciplines and to borrow what they could from the methodologies developed in such fields as experimental design, psychometrics, survey research, and ethnography. The results were disappointing and underscored the need for the development of new conceptualizations and methods tailored to fit the needs of evaluators more precisely. Scholars responded to this need, and by 1970 important seminal writings had provided conceptual foundations and scaffolding for the young field of evaluation (Cronbach, 1963; Scriven, 1967; Stake, 1967; Stufflebeam, 1968). Books of readings on evaluation were published (Caro, 1971; Worthen and Sanders, 1973). Articles about evaluation appeared with increasing frequency in professional journals. Together, these publications resulted in a proliferation of new evaluation models that collectively provided new ways of thinking about evaluation. This emerging body of literature showed evaluation to be a multidimensional technical and political enterprise that required both new conceptualizations and new insights into the ways in which methodologies borrowed from other fields could be used appropriately.

In recognizing the need for unique theories for evaluation, Shadish, Cook, and Leviton (1991, p. 31) noted that, "as evaluation matured, its theory took on its own special character that resulted from the interplay among problems uncovered by practitioners, the solutions they tried, and traditions of the academic discipline of each evaluator, winnowed by twenty years of experience."

Publications focusing exclusively on evaluation appeared in the 1970s. They included such journals and series as *Evaluation, Evaluation and Program Planning, Evaluation Practice, Educational Evaluation and Policy Analysis, New Directions for Program Evaluation,* and the *Evaluation Studies Review Annual.* The number of books published expanded markedly in the second half of the 1970s and throughout the 1980s. Textbooks, reference books, and even compendia and encyclopedias of evaluation all appeared. Clearly, the necessary conceptual underpinnings of a profession are accumulating in a body of evaluation literature that is arguably unique. Thus, evaluation seems to qualify as a profession on the second criterion: There is a body of knowledge that outlines the content of the field and its unique (or adapted) theories, strategies, and methods.

Programs for the Preparation of Evaluators

Foreseeing that education had few persons trained in educational inquiry skills, the U.S. Congress funded graduate training programs in educational research and evaluation in 1965. These programs included fellowship stipends for graduate study in these new specializations. Several universities launched full-fledged, federally funded graduate programs aimed at training educational evaluators. When federal funds disappeared, so did many of the graduate programs that they had supported. In 1971, graduate programs for training evaluators existed at more than a hundred American universities (Worthen and Byers, 1971). Fifteen years later, only forty-four U.S. universities had such programs (May, Fleischer, Scheirer, and Cox, 1986). And many programs that had had many courses in evaluation scaled back to a single elective course.

The evaluation preparation programs that continued generally offered training tailored to fit the reconceptualized views of evaluation that were emerging. Notions of how evaluators should be trained gradually expanded beyond traditional training. Courses in research design, statistics, and measurement were often supplemented by a wide variety of applied methods and techniques courses in such areas as naturalistic observation, interviewing techniques, content analysis, performance assessment, and communication and writing skills. Evaluation internships, assistantships, and practica became more central in preparation programs as evaluation mentors realized that, in evaluation as elsewhere, the best training is often apprenticeship training.

In recent years, the training of evaluators has increasingly been relocated to nonacademic settings. In-service evaluation training for practitioners is often offered in schools, state agencies, and businesses. On occasion, large corporations have established corporate training centers (such as Xerox Document University). These centers, which resemble miniuniversities, provide training in evaluation along with other techniques. Some of these centers award certificates attesting that the recipient is qualified in the specialization in which he or she has been trained. And, of course, many persons follow serendipitous career paths into evaluation roles where their preparation consists primarily of on-the-job bootstrapping. On balance, there are a sufficient number of evaluation training programs in universities, government agencies, corporations, and other settings to produce an ongoing supply of professional evaluators. It seems clear that evaluation meets this third criterion for having reached the status of a profession.

Stable Career Opportunities for Evaluators

One sign that a specialization is a profession is a continuing need for the services of personnel trained in that specialty. No field that is only a fad that flourishes briefly and then fades would qualify as a profession. In judging evaluation on this dimension, we must consider whether, despite uncertain social and economic trends, evaluation provides the stable employment opportunities that are typical of mature professions.

At first, evaluation seemed to be just another boom-and-bust specialty. When the need for evaluators grew quickly between 1965 and 1975, it seemed that evaluation training could provide stable career opportunities for anyone who developed a reasonable degree of expertise in evaluation. That view grew doubtful in the late 1970s, when a dip in the level of federal funding for evaluation appeared to signal a declining U.S. job market for evaluators. In the early 1980s, Ronald Reagan cast a darker shadow over the evaluation scene. Federal evaluation mandates were quietly shelved as the so-called new federalism reduced federal funding for education and other social programs and cut federal control over the ways in which states and local agencies spent the federal funds that they received. Much categorical funding that had required evaluation was replaced by block grants to states, which were largely exempt from evaluation requirements. Most analysts during the early 1980s were convinced that state and local agencies, hard pressed for operational funds, would use categorical funding to buy supplies, repair equipment, or add staff. Evaluation was predicted to be one of the major casualties of the Reagan administration: Since federal mandates had spawned evaluation in state and local agencies, it seemed reasonable to expect that evaluation would decline or even cease when federal evaluation requirements were relaxed or abolished.

By 1982, these pessimistic prophecies seemed to have proved accurate. Governmental monitoring of categorical funding programs was drastically reduced. Individual evaluators and evaluation agencies that depended on contracts with federal programs found this source of income drying up. For example, Shadish, Cook, and Leviton (1991) note that the number of evaluation studies conducted by the U.S. Office of Planning, Budget, and Evaluation dropped from 114 in 1980 to 11 in 1984. The declines in other evaluation activities that depended on federal funds were comparable.

Gloom soon spread over the evaluation landscape, and evaluators' conferences in the early and mid 1980s focused on such themes as the decline of evaluation. Evaluation trainers at many universities began to ask whether it was ethical to train neophytes in roles for which demand was thought to be diminishing. For a time, it seemed that the evaluation bubble had burst. Evaluation seemed destined for the graveyard of promising endeavors that had failed to fulfill their potential.

But the situation began to change. For reasons that at first could not be explained, some evaluation agencies seemed to be bucking the declining trends. Indeed, they found that the 1980s had brought a stronger surge of evaluation business than ever before, and soon they were eagerly seeking to add well-qualified evaluators to their staffs. Gradually, it became apparent that only the evaluation agencies that depended primarily on federal funds had been hard hit, while the agencies that served state and local agencies, corporations, professional associations, and the like were finding that evaluation was still a bustling, thriving enterprise.

Somehow—perhaps only the most sagacious historical analyst could determine all the causes—decision makers in state and local government, business, and industry had begun to use evaluation for their own purposes—to provide information that they needed to guide policy and program implementation. Gradually, increasing numbers of agencies began to commission evaluation studies not because they had been forced to but because they believed that the resulting data would be helpful. House (1990) noted this trend in the emerging tendency for large bureaucracies to develop their own evaluation offices, and Worthen and Seeley (1990) described how evaluation had been institutionalized by a variety of enterprises across broad sectors of contemporary society.

For those who recognized that this widespread institutionalization of evaluation would lend stability to the evaluation job market, the pessimism that had prevailed at the beginning of the decade soon passed. Openings for evaluators were appearing in a wide variety of settings, which included public and private school districts, state and regional education agencies, social service agencies, universities and colleges, state systems of higher education, test and text publishers, and the military, business, and industry. Evaluation academics were at first amused and then amazed as they saw their students recruited to evaluate personnel training programs run by large, national accounting firms, insurance and brokerage houses, and fast-food chains.

The shortage of trained evaluators is obvious today, as the traditional employers of evaluators are now forced to compete with such firms as Aetna,

Xerox, and Price Waterhouse. Every year, the number of evaluation vacancies outside academic settings surpasses the number of qualified candidates. And the surge in federal program evaluation over the past few years has accentuated the need for evaluators. Ginsburg, McLaughlin, and Takai (1992, p. 24) note that "spending on program evaluation by the U.S. Department of Education exceeds $40 million per year, a tripling of the budget over the last five years." So a career in evaluation seems again to be a very good possibility. If the probability of continued employment in a specialization is an important criterion for considering it to be a profession, evaluation may well be considered a viable profession.

Procedures for the Certification or Licensure of Evaluators

Since an extensive discussion of this question is beyond the scope of this chapter, I will only touch on it lightly. For this chapter, the central question is whether there are mechanisms for the certification or licensing of evaluators similar to those that mark teachers, psychologists, and certified public accountants as professionals. The answer, of course, is no.

Despite pleas that the American Educational Research Association establish mechanisms to provide certification for qualified evaluators (Gagne, 1975; Worthen, 1972), neither it nor any other association or agency has stepped forward to assume responsibility for the licensing or certification of evaluation practitioners. As a result, there is currently no way of preventing incompetent or unscrupulous operators from proclaiming themselves to be evaluators. Without some type of credentialing process, it is difficult for those who need evaluation services to determine in advance that those whom they select are indeed competent. "Let the buyer beware" is still the watchword for those who must retain the services of an evaluation specialist. In the absence of certification or licensure, unprincipled hucksters can do much mischief and in the process badly tarnish the image of evaluation.

Perhaps that cannot be helped. I am much less sanguine today that we can set up credentialing systems than I was two decades ago. However desirable it may be to have some way of ensuring that the unqualified cannot masquerade as evaluators, the development of such a mechanism does not seem feasible for two reasons. First, rooted as evaluation is in so many disciplines and with today's evaluators trained in as many diverse specializations and through such diverse means as they are, it is hard to imagine how any broad agreement about the essential elements of evaluation competencies could be forged. Put bluntly, since there is so little agreement about the methods and techniques that evaluators should use, it seems almost certain that a majority of practicing evaluators would reject an effort to construct and use a template of any sort to judge the qualifications of all evaluators. Second, it seems unlikely that any professional association or government agency will soon be equipped to grapple with the thorny and often litigious business of licensure or certification, especially in a field where those affected by the effort are more accustomed to evaluating than to being evaluated.

Nevertheless, until and unless we establish some feasible mechanism for ensuring that those who practice evaluation are competent to do so, evaluation cannot be considered a fully mature profession.

Development of Professional Associations for Evaluators

Several professional associations in North America have emerged to provide homes for evaluators. (Similar trends are seen in other countries.) One of the first North American efforts was not a full-blown association as such but rather Division H of the American Educational Research Association, which provided a home for school evaluators. However, two professional associations for practicing evaluators were founded in 1976. The Evaluation Network (EN) consisted largely of educational evaluators, while most members of the Evaluation Research Society (ERS) served in other professional fields.

In 1985, the EN and the ERS merged to form the American Evaluation Association (AEA), which, with about 2,200 members, is the largest professional association that exists solely to serve the needs of practicing evaluators. The Canadian Evaluation Society (CES) was launched to serve the needs of Canadian evaluation practitioners who worked in settings ranging from provincial ministries to private consulting groups. Given the scope and stature of these associations, it is clear that evaluators have viable professional organizations. On this criterion, evaluation fares as well as any profession.

Criteria for Determining Membership in Evaluation Associations

Most professions have established criteria for denying membership in professional associations to those who are patently unqualified in the business of the profession. This cannot be said of evaluation. The criteria for membership in all the professional evaluation associations just mentioned are lenient, and no organization would effectively exclude those who were not qualified as evaluators from membership. On this criterion, as on the criterion of certification, it appears that evaluation has not reached full maturity as a profession.

Influence of Evaluation Associations on Preparation Programs for Evaluators

In many professions, the major professional associations play a powerful role in shaping university preparation programs through accreditation or similar mechanisms. Evaluation associations exert no such influence. None of the professional associations for evaluators mentioned earlier exercise any direct control or influence over any preservice program that purports to train evaluators. The evaluation associations do not accredit preservice training programs or control decisions about required course content, essential internship experiences, or faculty qualifications. On this criterion, too, evaluation is not fully a profession.

Development of Standards for Evaluation Practice

Most professions contain technical standards, ethical standards, or both that are intended to ensure that professional practice is of high quality. Evaluation was without such standards during its early years. Then in 1981, evaluation took a giant step forward toward qualifying as a profession when several years of work by the Joint Committee on Standards for Educational Evaluation, a coalition of professional associations concerned with evaluation in education and psychology, resulted in the publication of *Standards for Evaluations of Educational Programs, Projects, and Materials* (Joint Committee on Standards for Educational Evaluation, 1981). These comprehensive standards were intended to guide both those who conducted evaluations and those who made use of evaluation reports.

In 1982, the ERS published another set of standards for evaluation practice (Rossi, 1982). Six years later, the Joint Committee on Standards for Educational Evaluation (1988) published the *Personnel Evaluation Standards*. Currently, the same organization is nearing the end of the process of revising the standards first published in 1981. If a set of standards to guide professional practice is a hallmark of a profession, then evaluation certainly qualifies, for its standards are much better developed than those now used to guide practice in several more venerable professions.

Profession, Professional Specialization, or Field of Professional Practice?

Up to this point, we have considered nine touchstones that seem useful in ascertaining whether a field of endeavor has attained the status of a distinct profession. Let us now consider these criteria together. What do they tell us about the progress of evaluation toward becoming a profession? Is evaluation separate and distinct from the other professions and disciplines with which it has been intertwined for decades? In short, is evaluation a profession?

The answer depends on the rigor with which we apply the nine criteria just examined. If an area of specialization must meet all nine criteria before it can be thought of as a profession, then evaluation is not a profession. Figure 1.1, which summarizes the preceding discussion of evaluation and the characteristics that most fully developed professions possess, shows that evaluation falls short on three. For evaluation to be considered a full-fledged profession,

Figure 1.1. Criteria for Judging Whether Evaluation
Has Become a Profession

Does Evaluation Meet the Criterion of:	Yes	No
1. A need for evaluation specialists?	√	
2. Content (knowledge and skills) unique to evaluation?	√	
3. Preparation programs for evaluators?	√	
4. Stable career opportunities in evaluation?	√	
5. Certification or licensure of evaluators?		√
6. Appropriate professional associations for evaluators?	√	
7. Exclusion of unqualified persons from those associations?		√
8. Influence of evaluators' associations on preservice preparation programs for evaluators?		√
9. Standards for the practice of evaluation?	√	

these three areas will need to be dealt with. Nevertheless, some conditions may be difficult ever to meet. For example, we may never resolve the challenge of certifying evaluators. Does this mean that evaluation will never qualify as a profession? Or can evaluation be considered a profession if it meets most of the criteria?

Those who have commented on the status of evaluation as a profession are not of one voice. A decade ago, most writers seemed to hold the view that evaluation had not yet attained the status of a distinct profession. For example, Rossi and Freeman (1993, p. 432) concluded that "evaluation is not a 'profession,' at least in terms of the formal criteria that sociologists generally use to characterize such groups. Rather, it can best be described as a 'near-group,' a large aggregate of persons who are not formally organized, whose membership changes rapidly, and who have little in common in terms of the range of tasks undertaken, competencies, work sites, and shared outlooks." Merwin and Weiner (1985) have also concluded that evaluators cannot yet claim full professional status.

Several recent authors have reached a somewhat more liberal conclusion. For example, Patton (1990) states unequivocally that evaluation has become a profession and that it is a demanding and challenging one at that. Shadish, Cook, and Leviton (1991, p. 25) are slightly more cautious: "Evaluation is a profession in the sense that it shares certain attributes with other professions and differs from purely academic specialties, such as psychology or sociology. Although they may have academic roots and members, professions are economically and socially structured to be devoted primarily to practical application of knowledge in a circumscribed domain with socially legitimated funding. . . . Professionals . . . tend to develop standards of practice, codes of ethics, and other professional trappings. Program evaluation is not fully professionalized, like medicine or the law; it has no licensure laws, for example. But it tends toward professionalization more than most disciplines."

To summarize, some now view evaluation as a profession because it possesses most of the touchstones that collectively define a profession. Others believe that evaluation is not now a full-blown profession and that it may never become one because it lacks licensure laws and some other characteristics of such professions as law and medicine. Perhaps evaluation will forever be a near-group that tends toward professionalization. Perhaps we may best describe it as a near-profession—an area of professional practice and specialization that has its own literature, its own preparation programs, its own standards of practice, and its own professional associations. Or perhaps evaluation is best viewed as a hybrid of profession and discipline that possesses many characteristics of both and lacks some essentials of each (Scriven, 1991; Worthen and Van Dusen, in press). Or perhaps the label that we give to the practice of evaluation is of less consequence than the ways in which we structure programs aimed at preparing competent evaluation practitioners.

Are Preparation Programs for Evaluation Practitioners Warranted?

It would matter little whether we considered evaluation to be a profession if it were not that our conceptions—and even our semantics—influence the ways in which we prepare personnel for evaluation roles. If we think of evaluation as a discipline, then we will expect preservice programs for evaluators to be patterned after those used to train academics in other disciplines. If we think of it as a profession, the course work and internships in our evaluator preparation programs will tend to resemble the methods courses and practica used to prepare practitioners for other professions. If we think of evaluation as a hybrid of discipline and profession, then our evaluation programs will combine elements of programs aimed at training practitioners with elements of programs used to prepare academics.

However we think of evaluation, this much is clear: Evaluation has matured rapidly during the past quarter century, and there is every indication that it will continue to develop and grow in the decades ahead. With its own journals, standards, and professional reference groups, evaluation has developed many of the important characteristics of a profession. And whether or not it can be considered a profession, it has emerged as an important area of specialization that demands uniquely prepared personnel if it is to reach its full potential. It has become institutionalized in many public and private sectors of our society, and, if evaluators are prepared to meet the challenge, evaluation can become one of the most useful and far-reaching areas of human endeavor. Against this backdrop, the present and potential importance of evaluation fully warrants a careful consideration of the issues and strategies involved in preparing evaluation specialists.

References

Caro, F. G. (ed.). *Readings in Evaluation Research*. New York: Sage, 1971.

Cronbach, L. J. "Course Improvement Through Evaluation." *Teachers College Record*, 1963, *64*, 672–683.

Gagne, R. M. "Qualifications of Professionals in Educational R&D." *Educational Researcher*, 1975, 4 (2), 7–11.

Ginsburg, A., McLaughlin, M., and Takai, R. "Reinvigorating Program Evaluation at the U.S. Department of Education." *Educational Researcher*, 1992, *21* (3), 24–27.

House, E. R. "Trends in Evaluation." *Educational Researcher*, 1990, *19* (3), 24–28.

Joint Committee on Standards for Educational Evaluation. *Standards for Evaluations of Educational Programs, Projects, and Materials*. New York: McGraw-Hill, 1981.

Joint Committee on Standards for Educational Evaluation. *The Personnel Evaluation Standards*. Newbury Park, Calif.: Sage, 1988.

May, R. M., Fleischer, M., Scheirer, C. J., and Cox, G. B. "Directory of Evaluation Training Programs." In B. G. Davis (ed.), *Teaching of Evaluation Across the Disciplines*. New Directions for Program Evaluation, no. 29. San Francisco: Jossey-Bass, 1986.

Merwin, J. C., and Weiner, P. H. "Evaluation: A Profession?" *Educational Evaluation and Policy Analysis*, 1985, 7 (3), 253–259.

Patton, M. Q. "The Challenge of Being a Profession." *Evaluation Practice*, 1990, *11* (1), 45–51.

Rossi, P. H. (ed.). *Standards for Evaluation Practice*. San Francisco: Jossey-Bass, 1982.

Rossi, P. H., and Freeman, H. E. *Evaluation: A Systematic Approach*. (5th ed.) Newbury Park, Calif.: Sage, 1993.

Scriven, M. "The Methodology of Evaluation." In R. E. Stake (ed.), *Curriculum Evaluation*. American Educational Research Association Monograph Series on Evaluation, no. 1. Chicago: Rand McNally, 1967.

Scriven, M. "Introduction: The Nature of Evaluation." *Evaluation Thesaurus*. (4th ed.) Newbury Park, Calif.: Sage, 1991.

Shadish, W. R., Jr., Cook, T. D., and Leviton, L. C. *Foundations of Program Evaluation*. Newbury Park, Calif.: Sage, 1991.

Stake, R. E. "The Countenance of Educational Evaluation." *Teachers College Record*, 1967, *68*, 523–540.

Stufflebeam, D. L. *Evaluation as Enlightenment for Decision Making*. Columbus: Ohio State University Evaluation Center, 1968.

Weiss, C. H. "Evaluating Social Programs: What Have We Learned?" *Society*, 1987, *25* (1), 40–45.

Wholey, J. E. "Using Evaluation to Improve Government Performance." *Evaluation Practice*, 1986, 7, 5–13.

Worthen, B. R. "Certification for Educational Evaluators: Problems and Potential." Paper presented at the annual meeting of the American Educational Research Association, Chicago, Apr. 15, 1972.

Worthen, B. R., and Byers, M. L. "An Exploratory Study of Selected Variables Related to the Training and Careers of Educational Research and Research-Related Personnel." Washington, D.C.: American Educational Research Association, 1971.

Worthen, B. R., and Sanders, J. R. *Educational Evaluation: Theory and Practice*. Belmont, Calif.: Wadsworth, 1973.

Worthen, B. R., and Sanders, J. R. *Educational Evaluation: Alternative Approaches and Practical Guidelines.* New York: Longman, 1987.

Worthen, B. R., and Sanders, J. R. "The Changing Face of Educational Evaluation." *Theory into Practice,* 1991, *30* (1), 3–12.

Worthen, B. R., and Seeley, C. "Problems and Potential in Institutionalizing Evaluation in State and Local Agencies." Paper presented at the annual meeting of the American Evaluation Association, Washington, D.C., Oct. 19, 1990.

Worthen, B. R., and Van Dusen, L. M. "The Nature of Evaluation." In H. Walbert (ed.), *International Encyclopedia of Education.* (2nd ed.) Oxford, England: Pergamon Press, in press.

BLAINE R. WORTHEN is professor and chair of the Research and Evaluation Methodology Program in the Department of Psychology at Utah State University and director of the Western Institute for Research and Evaluation in Logan, Utah.

The skills and knowledge that evaluators need include those bor-
rowed from other disciplines as well as those unique to the field of
evaluation. Inclusion of multiple perspectives in evaluator training
can help to develop the field and improve the practice of evaluation.

Training Evaluators: Unique Skills and Knowledge

Donna M. Mertens

Evaluators work in complex environments, such as enrichment programs for deaf, gifted adolescents; drug and alcohol abuse programs for the homeless; and management programs for high-level radioactive waste. The field of evaluation itself is evolving as it develops through the reflective practice of the professionals involved. Evaluators have an ethical responsibility to continue their education and keep up-to-date on developments in the field (Eastmond, 1991). In consequence of this assertion, I have written this chapter for students of evaluation, by whom I mean not only those who are enrolled in formal training programs but also all practicing evaluators and teachers of evaluation.

Perspectives and Assumptions

My answer to the question, What are the unique skills and knowledge that should be considered for the preparation of evaluators? is based on four assumptions. First, we live in a multicultural society, and I assume that evaluators must bring a sensitivity to multicultural issues and perspectives to their work. Beaudry (1992, p. 82) notes that program evaluators must seek to include the multiple perspectives of ethnicity, race, gender, social class, and persons with disabilities: "Program evaluation must take notice of the changes

I thank the following people for their comments on my draft framework: Jennifer Greene, Jody Fitzpatrick, Hallie Preskill, Nick Eastmond, Jack McKillip, Dianna Newman, and Terry Hedrick.

in our society and begin to respond to social issues represented by multicultural education. Hate crimes and ethnic strife are reported on the front pages of newspapers and in the courts and the schools as well as all around the world. In education, much of what we know about negative racial prejudice, biases in testing, culturally biased instructional materials, and teacher effects remains part of the hidden curriculum. Multicultural awareness and education have equal relevance for health care, business, and industry as these sectors of society cope with the shifting patterns of a culturally diverse work force."

Stanfield (1993, pp. 6–7) addresses the same point: "The dramatically changing world in which we live demands that we cease to allow well-worn dogma to keep us from designing research [read *evaluation*] projects that will provide the data necessary for the formulation of adequate explanations for the racial and ethnic dimensions of human life." Although the author just cited speaks from the context of ethnicity and social science research, his comments can be more broadly interpreted as suggesting that evaluators must rethink traditional methods in order to be responsive to such alternative perspectives as those of minorities, women, the poor, and persons with disabilities.

Evaluation literature is only beginning to address the feminist (Farley and Mertens, 1993; Mertens, 1992; Shapiro, 1987) and minority perspectives (Madison, 1992). However, students of evaluation can borrow from the research-based literature and create the applications and implications that are necessary. The perspective of persons with disabilities has not been addressed as fully in the research literature (Mertens and McLaughlin, in press) as the perspectives of other groups. I include them here because a growing literature suggests that they view themselves as an oppressed cultural group (Wilcox, 1989).

Second, I view evaluation as a unique discipline that has borrowed many skills and much knowledge from social science research. Evaluation is an emerging profession with an expanding body of skills and knowledge that require continual review. Skills are things that evaluators need to be able to do. Knowledge is things that evaluators need to know. The model that I propose combines skills and knowledge, because evaluators need to be able to apply what they know in order to conduct evaluations competently.

Third, I assume that a core set of skills and knowledge exists across disciplines for evaluators. The particular emphasis of the skills and knowledge required in specific contexts depends on the discipline in which the training occurs, the level of the training, the nature of the training (for example, degree or nonacademic program, single course or program, new training or continuing education), the area of application (for example, education, economics, psychology, criminal justice, public administration, business, health, sociology, social work), the nature of the organization that employs the evaluator, and the level of the position that he or she holds. Having asserted that there is a core set of skills and knowledge, I also want to recognize the dispute between proponents of the view that evaluation has content-specific knowledge and advocates of the generalist view. Eisner (1991) describes a connoisseur as an individual who is highly perceptive in one domain and able to make fine discriminations among complex and subtle qualities. I believe that evaluators need either to be connoisseurs in the area of application (for example, drug abuse, deafness) or to include a subject matter expert (connoisseur) in the planning, conduct, and interpretation of an evaluation.

Last, I assume also that evaluators must be capable of being responsive to the needs of the client. They must be capable of recommending the most appropriate approach to an evaluation problem. Some problems can best be studied with quantitative data, while others call for qualitative data. While individual evaluators may not be expert in all quantitative and qualitative research methods, they do need to be able to recommend the most appropriate approach. If necessary, they can work in a team with evaluators who have greater expertise in other methods. Sechrest (1992) argues that evaluators need increased sophistication in quantitative methods. I agree that there is room for experts in either quantitative or qualitative methods, but there is also a need for those who function comfortably in both domains. Lincoln and Guba (1992) argue that a mixture of quantitative and qualitative methods can be appropriate to any paradigm.

Methodology

I used a number of different techniques to identify the skills and knowledge unique to evaluation. I reviewed existing literature, such as textbooks on evaluation (Brinkerhoff, Brethower, Hluchyj, and Nowakowski, 1983; Popham, 1988; Shadish, Cook, and Leviton, 1991; Rossi and Freeman, 1993; Posavac and Carey, 1992; Worthen and Sanders, 1987), presentations on training at the annual meetings of the American Evaluation Association (Altschuld, 1992; Barrington, 1989; Covert, 1992; Eastmond, 1992; Mertens, 1992), literature identified through the use of ERIC and other data bases, training-related articles in the journal *Evaluation Practice,* the U.S. General Accounting Office (1991) performance appraisal system for evaluators, and Davis's (1986) volume on evaluation training. I also consulted other evaluators and reflected on my own experience as an evaluator trainer for twenty-plus years. I conducted a content analysis of the skills and knowledge that I found in these various sources and organized them into a conceptual framework. I shared this conceptual framework with evaluators and trainers in a variety of disciplines, including education, psychology, business, administration, government, and interdisciplinary programs.

Skills and Knowledge Needed

I have divided the skills and knowledge into four categories: those unique to evaluation, topics associated with typical training in the methodology of research and inquiry, topics in such related areas as political science or anthropology, and discipline-specific topics. I chose this organizational framework because it lends itself to the overall design of an evaluation training program. A student who enrolls in an evaluation training program typically also receives course work in research methodology, including research design, statistics, and measurement. This organizational framework suggests areas that need to be included in evaluation courses because they are not often taught elsewhere (the components of these other topic areas arising in evaluation are unique). It also suggests other disciplines that can provide a more complete training experience. Exhibit 2.1 displays the topics associated with research, related areas, and specific disciplines. Discussion of these topics is beyond the scope of this chapter.

I focus here on the unique skills and knowledge associated with evaluation. Standard evaluation textbooks typically cover some of these topics, and I will therefore not elaborate on them. I will discuss certain controversial and emerging topics in evaluation for three reasons. First, the standard textbooks typically do not discuss them at length. Second, students of evaluation should be aware of the controversies in the field. Third, I hope to push trainers to think of including emerging topics—that is, topics that are still developing and on which consensus has not yet developed—as valid for inclusion in the evaluation curriculum.

The skills and knowledge listed in Exhibit 2.1 can all be taught with special insights and examples from evaluation. However, certain topics are not generally covered in a course in research, related areas, or other disciplines. These topics are discussed in the sections that follow.

Introductory Information About Evaluation. Evaluation textbooks typically include information about the definition of evaluation, the reasons why evaluations are conducted, the various types of evaluations (for example, implementation, process, outcome, impact, formative, summative), trends affecting evaluation, the roles that evaluators can play (for example, external, internal), and the history of evaluation.

Philosophical Assumptions. Evaluation classes should teach the philosophical assumptions underlying the positivist and postpositivist paradigmatic orientations. Although these assumptions should be taught in the research methodology classes, the teacher of evaluation cannot safely assume that they will be (Lopez and Mertens, 1993). Lather (1992) proposed an organizing framework for paradigms that is relevant here: positivists who seek to predict; postpositivists who seek to understand (this group includes those whom the evaluation literature has labeled *interpretive, naturalistic,* and *constructivist*), and postpositivists who seek to emancipate (this group includes feminists and race-specific inquirers). For the reasons outlined in the section on perspectives and assumptions, I would add persons with disabilities to the emancipatory category. Guba and Lincoln (1989) have explained the assumptions underlying positivists and postpositivists (read *constructivists*) in detail, and the trainer of evaluation could follow up on emancipatory paradigms through such sources as Lather (1991), Farley and Mertens (1993), Harding (1993), Shapiro (1987),

Exhibit 2.1. Knowledge and Skills Associated with Evaluation

I. Knowledge and skills associated with research methodology

  A. Philosophical assumptions of alternative paradigms and perspectives, for example, positives and postpositivists (for example, constructivist; feminists, minorities, and persons with disabilities) (Lather, 1992)

  B. Methodological implications for alternative assumptions

  C. Planning and conducting research

    1. Literature review strategies

    2. Theoretical frameworks

    3. Hypothesis/questions formulation

    4. Research design (quantitative designs—for example, observational research, surveys, experimental, quasi-experimental, correlational, causal comparative, and single-subject—and internal and external validity qualitative designs—for example, case studies and ethnography—and trustworthiness; and mixed designs)

    5. Data collection strategies: sample selection, quantitative data collection (for example, test construction, reliability, validity, application of tests, norm-and criterion-referenced tests, selective measurement intruments, assessing measurement instruments, measurement error and bias interpreting test results, instrument construction); qualitative data collection (for example, observation, interviewing, focus groups, document review, unobtrusive measures)

    6. Data analysis and interpretation: data preparation; construction of data bases; handling missing data; computer usage for data analysis; statistical analysis; qualitative data analysis strategies; display of data; presentation of well-supported findings, conclusions, and recommendations; communicative results and follow-up

II. Knowledge and skills needed for evaluation but borrowed from other areas

  A. Administration/business

    1. Project management: making effective use of resources; organizing and conducting of meetings; developing and administering budgets; managing personnel; delegating work; supervising staff; reviewing work products; supervising and evaluating staff; promoting teamwork; observing equal opportunity principles

    2. Strategic planning

    3. Auditing and evaluation

    4. Evaluation and program development

  B. Communication/psychology

    1. Oral communication: communicating with staff, external agencies, general public, and the press; obtaining needed information skillfully; avoiding misunderstanding; projecting a positive image; using media appropriately in presentation; leading discussions; conducting productive meetings; handling hostility and controversy; seeking and respecting others viewpoints

    2. Written communication: writing status reports, one-page factual summaries, executive summaries, proposals, reports, briefing papers, memos, case studies, interview notes, testimony, data collection, instrument performance appraisals, speeches, and professional articles; using computer software to

Exhibit 2.1. *(continued)*

produce appropriate text and graphics; establishing feedback loops to avoid surprises and allow people to respond to drafts; providing constructive feedback on written products

3. People skills: getting along with people, logically explaining expectations, using sound judgment as to what should be said/written, counseling employees in need of remediation, resolving sensitive personnel problems, rewarding good performance, providing timely feedback

4. Negotiation: negotiating contract, evaluation questions; separating people from the problem, dealing with issues and values; focusing on many interests that are represented; inventing options for mutual gain (Barrington, 1989)

5. Personal qualities: credible, good judgment, flexible, sense of humor, continually learning, self-reflexive, curious about how things work, ability to show respect for the efforts of others

C. Philosophy

1. Ethics
2. Valuing: determining the value of an object, applying criteria to information about an object to arrive at a defensible value statement

D. Political science

1. Policy analysis
2. Legislation and evaluation: the place of evaluation in current legislation

E. Anthropology: cross-cultural skills

F. Economics (T. Hedrick, personal communication, July 9, 1993)

1. Cost-benefit and cost-effectiveness analysis; supply/demand theory; discounting; wage rate analysis
2. Controlling for economic factors, for example, changes in the unemployment rate

III. Knowledge and skills unique to specific disciplines

A. Education: educational objectives, instructional design, instructional product evaluation, teacher evaluation, populations with special needs, accreditation, alternative assessment strategies

B. Psychology: human development; social service programs; clinical models; goal attainment scaling; outcome evaluation of psychotherapeutic interventions; psychological measurement; work environment (motivation, job satisfaction, productivity) (Corday, Boruch, Howard, and Boozin, 1986)

C. Health: epidemiological studies

D. Business: task analysis; job analysis; management; organizational change; market research; organizational design and development; information systems; conflict resolution (Perloff and Rich 1986)

E. Government: policies, procedures, regulations, and legislation that apply to the work area (U.S. General Accounting Office, 1991)

F. Public administration: distinctions between the public and private sectors (for example, many "bosses" in the public sector; legislative, judicial, executive, public, special interest groups); no clear bottom line as with profit in the private sector; accountability to the public (J. Fitzpatrick, personal communication, July 8, 1993) and Nielsen (1990) for feminists; Madison (1992), Marin and Marin (1991), and Stanfield and Dennis (1993) for minorities; and Mertens and McLaughlin (in press) for persons with disabilities. Evaluation courses should include these diverse perspectives and should be integrated into the process of planning and implementing an evaluation on the understanding that an inquirer's philosophical assumptions and theoretical orientation influence every stage of the design process.

Theories and Models of Evaluation. Numerous methods for the organization of the many theories and models of evaluation have emerged. Shadish, Cook, and Leviton (1991) explore the knowledge base that has emerged regarding evaluation theories. Theories encompass the choice of evaluation method, philosophy of science, public policy, and value orientation. These authors have identified three stages of evaluation theories: theories that use a rigorous, scientific method and emphasize the search for "truth"; theories that emphasize the need for detailed knowledge about how organizations in the public sector work to increase the political and social usefulness of results; and theories that integrate alternatives generated in the first two stages. Guba and Lincoln (1989) provide a contrasting framework for theories and models of evaluation that includes four "generations": measurement (testing), description (objectives), judgment, and the responsive, constructivist theory of evaluation. As I mentioned in the preceding section, emerging theories associated with the emancipatory paradigm provide fertile ground for an exploration of the meaning of alternative perspectives and their methodological implications.

Planning and Conducting an Evaluation. Although the process of planning and conducting an evaluation varies with the theoretical framework, the student of evaluation should be knowledgeable about and able to apply the following steps:

1. Focusing the evaluation: This step includes identifying the object of the evaluation, its purpose, its audiences, and the constraints and opportunities. Identification and involvement of stakeholders have been tied to the increasing utilization of evaluation results, and they have also been a source of controversy in the evaluation field. Harding (1993) and Madison (1992) assert that the stakeholders involved should be those with the least power and that team-building and collaboration strategies should be devised to include clients in a meaningful way. T. Hedrick (personal communication, July 9, 1993) believes that team building is not appropriate in such settings as federal oversight evaluations. J. Greene (personal communication, July 7, 1993) believes that what is distinctive about evaluation is the way in which politics intertwines with public program and policy decisions and the distinctive, contested audiences of an evaluation. Students should explore who should be involved in an evaluation, whose purposes an evaluation should serve, and how best they can be appropriately involved.

2. Designing the evaluation and formulating questions: The choice of a theo-
    retical framework and evaluation model discussed previously guides the
    evaluator here.
3. Planning data collection: The evaluator needs to identify the information
    needs, sources of information, instruments (including ways to describe the
    program treatment and implementation), and ways to identify the theory
    of the program being evaluated (that is, the context and presuppositions of
    the organizations and groups involved).
4. Analyzing and interpreting data: The evaluator needs to identify appropri-
    ate analytical approaches for the type of data collected. Identifying them
    will provide a mechanism for accurate and meaningful interpretation.
5. Planning, reporting, and utilization: The evaluator needs to facilitate effec-
    tive communication and integrate utilization strategies throughout the eval-
    uation process.
6. Planning management: The evaluator needs to determine the resources
    required and the time line of activities.
7. Planning meta-evaluation: The evaluator needs to know how to evaluate
    the quality of the evaluation plan, process, and product.

Students should be given the opportunity to implement their evaluation
plans through small evaluation projects completed as a class project or as a part
of an internship. Several authors have provided helpful hints concerning the
inclusion of practical experiences in training programs (Eastmond, Saunders,
and Merrell, 1989; Morris, 1989; Preskill, 1992).

Socialization into the Profession. Students of evaluation should be
given the opportunity to become socialized into the profession by means of
involvement with professional organizations, networking with evaluators, and
interacting with the evaluation literature.

Special Topics in Evaluation. The following topics are very important
in evaluation and should be included in the preparation of evaluators:

1. Ethics: professional behavior, use of information, confidentiality, sensitivity
    to effect on others, pressure from client to distort facts, proper response to
    discovering information that is morally or legally volatile, and so on (Mor-
    ris and Cohn, 1992)
2. Standards for evaluation of programs and personnel (Joint Committee on
    Standards for Educational Evaluation, 1981, 1988)
3. Politics of evaluation: knowing the players, the policy environment, the
    power of communication, how to get people to come to an agreement, and
    how people are likely to use information (Barrington, 1989); knowing how
    organizations work, how to understand an organization's goals and inter-
    nal and external forces (that is, how to analyze its political context) (H.
    Preskill, personal communication, June 23, 1993)

4. Specific methods and contexts, such as needs assessment (McKillip, 1987); evaluability assessment; futuring (the field of future studies) (Patton, 1990); and international evaluations
5. Evaluator as trainer: training evaluation clients and users

The section in Exhibit 2.1 on skills and knowledge borrowed from related areas includes other topics, such as policy analysis, communication skills, and cost analysis, that are essential to the preparation of evaluators.

Summary

The training of evaluators should reflect the evolving, dynamic nature of the field of evaluation. Many core topics identified here are reflected in evaluation textbooks. Evaluation also borrows skills and knowledge from other disciplines, but a training program for evaluators should examine them specifically through an evaluation lens. The inclusion of emerging topics in an evaluation training program can sensitize students of evaluation to these issues and make them better able to serve the people whom their evaluations affect. The training of evaluators should prepare them to reflect on and engage in dialogue about the best ways of responding to society's diverse demands. The field of evaluation needs to think in terms of multiple, not singular, perspectives when it trains evaluators.

References

Altschuld, J. W. "Structuring Programs to Prepare Professional Evaluators." Paper presented at the annual meeting of the American Evaluation Association, Seattle, Wash., 1992.

Barrington, G. V. "Evaluator Skills Nobody Taught Me, or What's a Nice Girl Like You Doing in a Place Like This?" Paper presented at the annual meeting of the American Evaluation Association, San Francisco, 1989.

Beaudry, J. S. "Synthesizing Research in Multicultural Teacher Education: Findings and Issues for Evaluation of Cultural Diversity." In A. Madison (ed.), Minority Issues in Program Evaluation. New Directions for Program Evaluation, no. 53. San Francisco: Jossey-Bass, 1992.

Brinkerhoff R. O., Brethower, D. M., Hluchyj, T., and Nowakowski, J. R. Program Evaluation. Boston: Kluwer Academic Press, 1983.

Cordray, D., Boruch, R., Howard, K., and Bootzin, R. "Teaching of Evaluation in Psychology: Northwestern University." In B. G. Davis (ed.), The Teaching of Evaluation Across the Disciplines. New Directions for Program Evaluation, no. 29. San Francisco: Jossey-Bass, 1986.

Covert, R. W. "Successful Competencies in Preparing Professional Evaluators." Paper presented at the annual meeting of the American Evaluation Association, Seattle, Wash., 1992.

Davis, B. G. "Overview of the Teaching of Evaluation Across the Disciplines." In B. G. Davis (ed.), The Teaching of Evaluation Across the Disciplines. New Directions for Program Evaluation, no. 29. San Francisco: Jossey-Bass, 1986.

Eastmond, J. N., Jr. "Addressing Ethical Issues When Teaching Evaluation." Paper presented at the annual meeting of the American Evaluation Association, Chicago, 1991.

Eastmond, J. N., Jr. "Structuring a Program to Prepare Professional Evaluators." Paper presented at the annual meeting of the American Evaluation Association, Seattle, Wash., 1992.

Eastmond, J. N., Jr., Saunders, W., and Merrell, D. "Teaching Evaluation Through Paid Contractual Arrangements." *Evaluation Practice,* 1989, *10* (2), 58–62.

Eisner, E. W. *The Enlightened Eye.* New York: Macmillan, 1991.

Farley, J., and Mertens, D. M. "The Feminist Voice in Evaluation Methodology." Paper presented at the annual meeting of the American Evaluation Association, Dallas, 1993.

Guba, E., and Lincoln, Y. S. *Fourth-Generation Evaluation.* Newbury Park, Calif.: Sage, 1989.

Harding, S. "Rethinking Standpoint Epistemology: 'What Is Strong Objectivity?'" In L. Alcoff and E. Potter (eds.), *Feminist Epistemology.* New York: Routledge, 1993.

Joint Committee on Standards for Educational Evaluation. *Standards for Evaluations of Educational Programs, Projects, and Materials.* New York: McGraw-Hill, 1981.

Joint Committee on Standards for Educational Evaluation. *The Personnel Evaluation Standards.* Newbury Park, Calif.: Sage, 1988.

Lather, P. *Getting Smart: Feminist Research and Pedagogy with/in the Postmodern.* New York: Routledge, 1991.

Lather, P. "Critical Frames in Educational Research: Feminist and Poststructural Perspectives." *Theory into Practice,* 1992, *31* (2), 1–12.

Lincoln, Y. S., and Guba, E. G. "In Response to Lee Sechrest's 1991 AEA Presidential Address: 'Roots: Back to Our First Generations,' Feb. 1991, 1–7." *Evaluation Practice,* 1992, *13* (3), 165–170.

Lopez, S. D., and Mertens, D. M. "Current Practices: Integrating the Feminist Perspective in Educational Research Classes." Presentation at the annual meeting of the American Educational Research Association, Atlanta, Ga., 1993.

McKillip, J. *Need Analysis.* Newbury Park, Calif.: Sage, 1987.

Madison, A. M. (ed.). *Minority Issues in Program Evaluation.* New Directions in Program Evaluation, no. 53. San Francisco: Jossey-Bass, 1992.

Marin, G., and Marin, B. V. *Research with Hispanic Populations.* Newbury Park, Calif.: Sage, 1991.

Mertens, D. M. "Structuring a Program to Prepare Professional Evaluators: What Aren't We Talking About (That We Should Be)?" Paper presented at the annual meeting of the American Evaluation Association, Seattle, Wash., 1992.

Mertens, D. M., and McLaughlin, J. *Research Methods in Special Education.* Newbury Park, Calif.: Sage, in press.

Morris, M. "Field Experiences in Evaluation Courses." In D. M. Mertens (ed.), *Creative Ideas for Teaching Evaluation.* Norwell, Mass.: Kluwer, 1989.

Morris, M., and Cohn, R. "Program Evaluators and Ethical Challenges: A National Survey." Paper presented at the annual meeting of the American Evaluation Association, Seattle, Wash., 1992.

Nielsen, J. M. (ed.). *Feminist Research Methods.* Boulder, Colo.: Westview Press, 1990.

Patton, M. Q. "The Challenge of Being a Profession." *Evaluation Practice,* 1990, *11* (1), 45–51.

Perloff, R., and Rich, R. F. "The Teaching of Evaluation in Schools of Management." In B. G. Davis (ed.), *The Teaching of Evaluation Across the Disciplines.* New Directions for Program Evaluation, no. 29. San Francisco: Jossey-Bass, 1986.

Popham, W. J. *Educational Evaluation.* Englewood Cliffs, N.J.: Prentice Hall, 1988.

Posavac, E. J., and Carey, R. J. *Program Evaluation: Method and Case Studies.* (4th ed.) Englewood Cliffs, N.J.: Prentice Hall, 1992.

Preskill, H. "Students, Client, and Teacher: Observations from a Practicum in Evaluation." *Evaluation Practice,* 1992, *13* (1), 39–46.

Rossi, P., and Freeman, H. E. *Evaluation: A Systematic Approach.* (5th ed.) Newbury Park, Calif.: Sage, 1993.

Sechrest, L. "Roots: Back to our First Generations." *Evaluation Practice,* 1992, *13* (1), 1–8.

Shadish, W. R., Jr., Cook, T. D., and Leviton, L. C. *Foundations of Program Evaluation: Theories of Practice.* Newbury Park, Calif.: Sage, 1991.

Shapiro, J. P. "Collaborative Evaluation: Toward a Transformation of Evaluation for Feminist Programs and Projects." Paper presented at the annual meeting of the American Educational Research Association, Washington, D.C., 1987.

Stanfield, J. H. "Methodological Reflections." In J. H. Stanfield II and R. M. Dennis (eds.), *Race and Ethnicity in Research Methods*. Newbury Park, Calif.: Sage, 1993.

Stanfield, J. H., II, and Dennis, R. M. (eds.). *Race and Ethnicity in Research Methods*. Newbury Park, Calif.: Sage, 1993.

U.S. General Accounting Office. *Performance Appraisal System of Band I, II, and III Employees*. Washington, D.C.: U.S. General Accounting Office, 1991.

Wilcox, S. "STUCK in School: Meaning and Culture in a Deaf Education Classroom." In S. Wilcox (ed.), *American Deaf Culture*. Burtonsville, Md.: Linstock Press, 1989.

Worthen, B. R., and Sanders, J. R. *Educational Evaluation*. New York: Longman, 1987.

DONNA M. MERTENS is professor in the Department of Educational Foundations and Research at Gallaudet University in Washington, D.C.

*The current status of evaluation as a profession is examined, and
two certification approaches for evaluation are described.*

Should Evaluators Be Certified?

Arnold J. Love

Certification is one serious issue that faces the field of evaluation. Currently,
anyone can assert that he or she is an evaluator and seek consulting assignments or employment. The client, who may know little about evaluation, has
the responsibility for sifting the wheat from the chaff. National and regional
evaluation groups in the United States and Canada have no mechanisms for
ensuring and maintaining the competence of evaluators or the quality of evaluation practice.

Both the American Evaluation Association (AEA) and the Canadian Evaluation Society (CES) see promoting evaluation as a profession to be a key ele-
ment of their missions (Canadian Evaluation Society Standards Development
Committee, 1992; House, 1993; Patton, 1990). In today's service economy,
being a professional means dedicating oneself to high standards of performance, not just being a member of a group that has been classified as a profession (Brody, 1989). Both the AEA and the CES face similar problems
concerning how to develop evaluation as a profession and promote an appropriate level of professionalism. The fundamental question is this: Should evaluators be certified and, if the answer is yes, by what process?

The essence of certification involves the assessment by professional peers
of the applicant's competence against standards accepted within the profession. The successful applicant then receives a written certificate from a recognized body, usually a professional association.

First, I will examine the developmental steps leading to the creation of a
new profession. They provide a context for an examination of the readiness of
the evaluation profession for certification. Then I will introduce two major

The opinions expressed in this chapter do not represent the position of the Canadian Evaluation Society.

NEW DIRECTIONS FOR PROGRAM EVALUATION, no. 62, Summer 1994   © Jossey-Bass Publishers approaches to certification: the professional development approach and the licensing approach. Finally, I will describe some experimental efforts to establish the foundations for a certification program and several scenarios of the way in which a feasible certification program could evolve.

Development of a Profession

The normal rule of the marketplace is that a primary relationship exists between buyer and seller and that the buyer has the responsibility for judging the quality of the goods or services that he or she proposes to purchase. Buyers vary in their ability to judge quality. In contrast, the professions seek to replace the warning "Let the buyer beware" with the guarantee "Let the buyer trust." Developing public trust in a profession is an interactive process that involves both the behavior of individual practitioners and systematic efforts by members of the profession to establish structural characteristics for its practice (Austin, 1981).

Moore (1970) suggests that creating the structure of a new profession has six steps: occupation, calling, organization, education, service orientation, and autonomy. I review each of these steps in the paragraphs that follow. They provide a useful context for understanding the place of certification in the development of a new profession and for an assessment of the feasibility of certification for evaluators.

Occupation. An occupation is a distinct and related set of activities. Deriving one's principal source of income from the practice of an occupation distinguishes the professional from the amateur. The ability of a professional to earn the majority of his or her income from an occupation often indicates exceptional competence and an occupational commitment. However, this characteristic is not universal, since some occupations (for example, "starving artist") may have insufficient demand or payment for their services, and virtually all occupations suffer competition from skilled amateurs and part-time practitioners.

Calling. A profession begins to transcend an occupational specialty when its members share a sense of vocation, that is, a sense of an inner calling to become part of a select professional group. Commitment to a vocation involves acceptance of the norms and standards of the profession and a close identification with professional peers. Professions usually forge and test this commitment during an intense period of training and socialization, which often requires an apprenticeship to experienced members of the profession.

Organization. Shared occupational interests and a sense of calling stimulate the formation of occupational organizations, such as professional associations, craft guilds, or unions. A hallmark of a profession is a strong, formal organization that considers the standards of competence and performance for its practitioners.

Education. Many occupations, especially those with the status of professions, demand formal educational qualifications. Professions ordinarily require that the type and quality of education received distinguishes the person with formal training from the person who has simply had experience in the occupation. For most professions, this demand usually means graduate training in a specialized school or program, although new or emerging professions (for example, computer programming) often prove to be exceptions.

Service Orientation. A distinguishing characteristic of a profession is a service orientation. Professions foster a service orientation by establishing three sets of rules: rules of competence, rules of performance, and rules of loyalty or service. For example, the professions foster competence and protect against incompetence by controlling admission and by setting standards for ongoing professional development (rule of competence). Competent professionals are expected to provide their clients with high-quality performance (rule of performance). To ensure high-quality performance, the professions establish and enforce performance standards and ethical codes. Finally, professions promote the norms of loyalty and service as a covenant of trust guaranteeing that the client's interests will be protected in any transaction with a professional (rule of service).

Autonomy. Modern professions are characterized by a high degree of technical specialization. As a result, there is widespread belief that only a specialist can judge the work of another specialist in the same field. At the final stage of its maturity, a profession typically asserts its autonomy by obtaining public or governmental cooperation to control access to the profession and enforce its performance standards and ethical codes through licensing statutes. The professions make use of government sanctions to protect the public while reducing competition by controlling access to their ranks. For the government, such a mechanism is useful for regulating highly specialized professions and protecting the public interest.

Is Evaluation Ready for Certification?

There are indications that evaluation is emerging as an occupational specialty with its own knowledge base, training programs, and professional associations. The last twenty-five years have seen the steady growth of evaluation as a discipline and as a field of professional practice. There are academic training programs in evaluation and a vast body of literature that includes scholarly journals, books, monographs, articles, and reports. In North America, the AEA and the CES together serve more than 3,500 members. Professional associations are being or have been organized in southeast Asia (Australasian Evaluation Society) and Europe. Overall, the demand for evaluation is increasing.

Although these developments are encouraging, do they indicate that evaluation has evolved to the point where it is ready for certification? My perception is that three key areas require closer attention before we can answer this question: the recognition of professional qualifications, the setting of standards, and the establishment of a code of ethics.

Recognition of Professional Qualifications. A professional association controls entry into a profession by setting minimum levels of qualification. It encourages professionalism among its members by recognizing their learning and professional development achievements.

The setting of minimum qualifications is problematic for the field of evaluation. The older professions (for example, medicine, law, psychology, economics) have comfortable homes in academic disciplines, professional schools, or both. Career paths and training programs have been established. In contrast, evaluation is largely an interdisciplinary, applied field without a home in any specific academic department (Bickman, 1990). Academic training programs that grant professional degrees in evaluation are limited.

Moreover, the evaluators who identify strongly enough with the profession to be members of the AEA or the CES are diverse in terms of their training, earned degrees, years of experience in evaluation, organizational affiliations, and evaluation responsibilities. Very few members have been formally trained as evaluators, and many practice part-time or have short-term responsibilities as evaluators. Evaluators are so diverse that Morell (1990) views evaluation as a loose coalition of dedicated practitioners, not as a cohesive discipline.

Institutionalization—a major force that is transforming all professions in North America—also is transforming evaluation. The majority of evaluators do not work as independent professionals but rather as employees who are part of a larger institution or bureaucracy. The necessary qualifications differ significantly depending on whether the evaluator is an academic, an independent contractor, or the employee of an organization. If we agree with Patton (1990) that the terms *professional evaluator* and *evaluation profession* should include external and internal evaluators, full- and part-time evaluators, and anyone who engages seriously in evaluation, then our certification efforts must be inclusive rather than exclusive.

This situation concerning qualifications is not unusual for a young profession. However, it does have a serious impact on the design and feasibility of any certification process.

Setting Standards. Over the last decade, four major organizations have proposed evaluation standards: The Joint Committee on Standards for Educational Evaluation (1981), the Evaluation Research Society Standards Committee (1982), the Comptroller General of the United States (1988), and the Office of the Comptroller General (1989) of Canada. Although the need for evaluation standards is widely recognized, there is at present no universally accepted set of standards to guide evaluation practice.

Professional associations adopt standards for several reasons. Standards can be powerful tools for ensuring the quality of services, clarifying and promoting the professional identity of a profession's members, and encouraging continuous professional development. They can also help consumers to select competent practitioners and preferred evaluation practices, and they can protect the public against incompetent practitioners and unethical practices.

There are drawbacks to the adoption of standards. Standards reflect the shared values of the profession. Given the diversity of evaluation practice, it may not be possible to agree on a common set of values that can be defined clearly enough to guide practice (Lincoln, 1985; McKillip and Garberg, 1986; Raven, 1984). Vague generalities quickly erode the credibility of a profession. Moreover, standards define not only our profession but also our roles as evaluators, our methods of working, and the latitude of our individual choice and innovation. Poorly conceived standards may do more to hinder than to help an emerging profession.

Despite the potential obstacles, it seems likely that the evaluation field soon will arrive at a workable set of standards. In its recent review of the major existing evaluation standards, the Canadian Evaluation Society Standards Development Committee (1992) decided that it was possible to create a set of standards that covered all key aspects of evaluation. Feedback from consultation sessions has shown that the current work of the joint committee in revising its standards also holds significant promise for the development of broadly applicable and widely supported evaluation standards.

Establishing a Code of Ethics. Standards of practice are not the same as ethical codes or principles (Brown and Newman, 1992). Although standards can address ethical issues to some degree, they serve as guidelines for practice, not as ethical principles.

At present, there is no accepted code of ethics or ethical principles for evaluators. The literature concerning ethical practice in evaluation is sparse. Given the varied educational backgrounds and professional affiliations of evaluators, they may practice under several different and potentially conflicting ethical codes.

Nevertheless, there are hopeful signs that a proactive and useful code of ethics for evaluation will be adopted in the near future. An AEA task force on guiding principles for evaluators recently produced a draft document and solicited extensive feedback regarding the principles proposed. The CES has undertaken a similar effort, and a discussion paper concerning a code of ethics and its relation to the profession of evaluation (Hurteau and Trahan, 1993) has been completed.

Two Approaches to Certification: Professional Development and Regulation

There are two distinct and complementary ways of viewing certification that are reflected in the definition of the word itself. *Certify* has its origins in a Latin word meaning "to make certain." To certify is to declare that something is certain or true by way of a formal statement, often in writing. One meaning of *certify* is to guarantee that something has value or worth, as in the expressions "certify a document" and "certify a check." Another meaning is to "issue a license to someone."

The professional development approach to certification reflects the first meaning of the word *certify*: Under this approach, certification verifies an individual's knowledge, competencies, and application of the profession's standards of practice and code of ethics. The second meaning of *certify* reflects the regulatory approach: That is, under this alternative approach, *certification* means licensing a person to practice a profession.

The professional development approach emphasizes that the central purpose of certification is to provide assurance of the quality of professional practice. Certification gives all parties confidence that the knowledge, skills, and practice of a certified professional meet high professional standards. It protects the client, the public, and the profession itself against the damage that can arise from incompetent and unethical practice by providing a yardstick against which individual competence can be judged. Certification also enhances the credibility, respect, and status accorded to certified professionals.

Another way of protecting consumers from incompetent and unethical practices is by certifying practitioners and granting licenses to practice. Licensing involves the development of public or governmental sanctions that make performance of the activities of the profession without the proper credentials a crime (Merwin and Weiner, 1985). To license, the professional association must first obtain legal authority to regulate the profession. Through licensing, the professional association then uses its legal power and responsibility to admit members to the profession and to enforce standards and ethical codes by applying sanctions.

The United States has a precedent for the regulatory certification—that is, licensing—of educational evaluators (Hoffman, 1982). In 1981, the Louisiana Board of Elementary and Secondary Education undertook to certify program evaluators, and it used the Joint Committee's standards (Joint Committee on Standards for Educational Evaluation, 1981) to ensure quality in the conduct of evaluations. The Louisiana State Department of Education undertook to provide evaluators with training in evaluation skills and technical assistance.

In my judgment, the regulatory approach to certification has several drawbacks at this point in time. First, licensing standards generally set minimum levels of quality in a profession's services. At this stage of its development, evaluation would be better served by ideal standards of excellence that promoted high-quality evaluations than by minimum standards.

Second, the scarcity of formal evaluation training programs makes meaningful control of professional training difficult. The alternative, exemplified by Louisiana, is to regulate specific types of evaluators—in this case, educational evaluators—through a state or provincial body that also assumes responsibility for training and technical support. The interdisciplinary and applied nature of evaluation, the diverse backgrounds and work situations of evaluators, and the loyalties of many evaluators to their primary disciplines make the control of admission and qualifying standards problematic at best and arrogant at worst.

Finally, it is costly to administer a licensing program. To fund such a program, evaluation would have to find sponsors, or evaluation organizations would have to require their members to pay substantially higher dues.

Exploring Feasible Models of Certification

The search for a feasible model of evaluation certification required countless hours of dialogue with evaluation clients and with colleagues in the AEA and the CES and several experiments by the CES to explore the parameters of a certification program. In many respects, the proposed model adopts the professional development approach rather than the regulatory one.

The professional development approach has several practical advantages. It permits the certification of persons with diverse disciplinary training and disciplinary loyalties while affirming unique competencies in evaluation. Moreover, adoption of a professional development approach permits the use of a flexible combination of formal and informal preparation methods. Efforts by the evaluation associations to develop a certification program based on competencies, if nothing else, will help greatly to clarify the professional identity of evaluators and stimulate increased inclusiveness.

In contrast to the purely regulatory approach, the professional development approach can be implemented almost immediately and evolve with the field. It permits the certification of individuals whose evaluation responsibilities may be limited (basic certification) as well as of evaluation specialists (intermediate and advanced certification). However, all certified evaluators must adhere to a common set of ethical guidelines and demonstrate a common set of core competencies. The professional development approach also gives all evaluators an incentive to upgrade their knowledge and skills continuously by recognizing and rewarding their efforts.

Such a model provides a practical and sound developmental path that will create a solid foundation if our professional associations choose at some future time to replace it with a regulatory model. The developmental path begins with a certificate program, then progresses to an accreditation program, and finally advances to regulation through licensing. The sections that follow describe some experimental work in the creation of foundations for certification and sketch scenarios for future implementation.

Certificate Program. A needs assessment indicated that about one-third of the members of the CES Ontario chapter required training in basic evaluation knowledge (for example, principles of evaluation design) and skills (for example, basic questionnaire construction). In response to these findings, the professional development committee of the Ontario chapter designed and pilot tested a set of four one-day courses providing a systematic introduction to program evaluation for new evaluators and a review and update for experienced evaluators.

The instructors for this series of courses were highly qualified university-level faculty who also were experienced evaluators. They had the task of blending relevant theory with their first-hand knowledge of evaluation as applied to a wide range of programs and then of using adult education techniques to deliver each course. Thumbnail sketches of the courses follow.

Understanding Program Evaluation. The first course, a general overview, was designed to familiarize participants with the key terms and concepts of evaluation. It addressed the benefits of program evaluation, basic steps in the evaluation process, and major theoretical approaches to program evaluation. It discussed the identification of stakeholders and their information needs, the fundamentals of evaluation design, and the various strategies for the collection and analysis of data. Reducing resistance to evaluation, involving staff and consumers in the evaluation process, evaluating with limited resources, increasing evaluation utilization, evaluation ethics, and reporting evaluation results were also included.

Building an Evaluation Framework. The second course dealt with basic concepts of needs assessment. Among these concepts were identifying the client and client needs, major approaches to the assessment of client needs, and evaluation methods that allow evaluators to get close to the client. The course also dealt with the issues of building an evaluation framework through logic models and program descriptions; involving managers and staff in the development of an evaluation framework; relating program design to client needs; defining program components; formulating indicators for program success; and using the evaluation framework for linking program performance with client needs.

Improving Program Performance. The third course focused on the use of evaluation as a management tool that can improve program performance and enhance internal accountability. Its content dealt with the following issues: monitoring and process evaluations, monitoring program performance with existing administrative data and information systems, and designing process evaluations. Identifying duplicated services, developing ongoing data collection instruments and procedures, clarifying the roles of key players, facilitating teamwork, and encouraging effective communication were also discussed. Information about linking process evaluation with program decision making, assessing client satisfaction, understanding continuous quality improvement, and using program evaluation for improving program quality and building a learning organization was incorporated into the content.

Evaluating for Results. The last course in the series addressed the definition of program results. The evaluation of results, ways of achieving a balance between flexibility and accountability, the development of result measures, and the design of outcome evaluations were some of its key aspects. Validity, reliability, and the appropriate use of quantitative, qualitative, and program-monitoring techniques were included. The course also addressed the topics of relating program results to program costs, understanding program benefits, measuring program equity and responsiveness to community needs, cost-benefit analysis, communicating evaluation findings, and using evaluations to improve program effectiveness and accountability.

The four courses were subsequently pilot tested in other provinces and territories with various types of participants (for example, academics, government employees, internal evaluators). The resulting evaluations, which have been encouraging, form the basis for our plan to change and expand the series, perhaps to five courses, and to offer a certificate to those who complete the series successfully.

The professional development committee of the CES is currently working on a two-year plan to develop and pilot test a core curriculum. The CES plans to develop an instructor's guide for local instructors, an instructor's workbook of case studies from various areas of application (for example, health, education, government services), a participant's manual, and a resource package for participants.

One action now under consideration is to have the courses delivered by experienced evaluators through a variety of educational venues, including community colleges, universities, continuing education, distance education, and independent study with a tutor and feedback. The CES would approve the courses and the instructors. The CES also would provide input concerning the required and optional courses needed to qualify for the certificate. This system would be flexible, and the CES would accept differences in credit value among institutions, substitutions of courses between institutions, and/or exemptions. This system could be managed through part-time paid staff at the CES national office. The applicants would pay a nominal fee to cover administrative costs.

Accreditation Program. Recently, the Canadian Evaluation Society completed a study relating the tasks that evaluators perform with the knowledge and skills required to perform them (Caron, 1993). The results of this study were used to generate a list of specific competencies that could be linked to particular training modules. The CES is working on a code of ethics and exploring the feasibility of setting principles and standards for the practice of evaluation in Canada. All these components are necessary before the CES can contemplate an accreditation program.

In the future, the CES may consider a bona fide accreditation program based on competencies, a code of ethics, and standards. The accreditation program would be a service to our members that would encourage the professional development of evaluation practitioners. The major target groups for the program would be persons who were preparing for a career in the evaluation field and current practitioners who wanted to increase their formal knowledge of evaluation and their qualifications.

The accreditation program would provide members of the association with a way of planning and organizing their personal development in the evaluation profession. The program would use a certificate of achievement to recognize individual efforts in the areas of personal learning activities, professional activities, and work experience in evaluation.

The accreditation program would give the CES an opportunity to measure evaluators' current competence against the standards of professional competence—the knowledge and skills needed to be an effective evaluation professional. The competencies serve as a guide in planning career growth and development. An accreditation review committee composed of peers would award certificates at basic, intermediate, and advanced levels. Only CES members in good standing would be awarded a certificate.

The approach just outlined has several advantages. Accreditation validates professional development achievements and areas of competence. It helps employers or clients to determine the level of competencies that evaluators need. It gives the individual evaluator a basis for developing his or her own professional development plan by indicating areas for further development in relation to personal and organizational needs. The awarding of accreditation certificates recognizes learning and the achievement of competence. The certificate enhances the evaluator's credibility with employers, clients, and colleagues, and it gives employers and clients a way of comparing and selecting candidates on the basis of their level of accreditation.

Regulating the Profession.

If the AEA and the CES wish to pursue the regulatory form of certification at some point in time, how might it happen? Here is one approach to the development of a certification program that licenses program evaluators:

Once the association has adopted a set of standards, a code of ethics, and a training program that reaches all its members and decides to seek legal control over the evaluation field, it would apply, under the legislation in force that governs professions, to become a legal body with the authority to govern and censure its members with respect to competence, ethics, and professional standards. It might also want to ask for the right to grant qualified members the exclusive use of a unique designation, such as *certified program evaluator*.

Licensing would be an extension of the association's current professional development program, and the process would resemble that in force in other self-regulating professions. Evaluation professionals who wished to be certified through the program would be required to complete successfully a written examination on the theories, concepts, and practices of the profession; to complete successfully a demonstration of a skill component, such as the design of an evaluation; to adhere to the association's code of ethics; and to make a commitment to continuous learning and to maintaining membership in the professional association.

It is not likely that efforts to legitimize the profession in any way that involves proprietary rights on labels like *program evaluation* will be successful. In the past, states have had difficulties with the licensing of psychotherapy because the activity was so general that the legislation became too restrictive. For example, clergy could not talk to members of their congregation about problems. The solution was to license disciplines, not activities. That solution may not work in program evaluation, since the field does not yet have a clear disciplinary basis in universities.

Conclusion

At their inception, professions organize around common occupational interests. During the growth phase, they develop standards of performance and quality. At maturity, they control access to their ranks. Before we can seriously entertain the idea of certification for evaluators, the associations that represent the profession must demonstrate leadership by defining their expectations for the field and then working to create that future. The professional associations must have the collective will to make good on their strategic plans to strengthen the profession of evaluation and to develop standards of practice, codes of ethics, and professional development programs for both new and experienced evaluators. Members of the associations, their employers and clients, and the public must all take part in this process.

References

Austin, D. "Comments on the Preceding Article: The Development of Clinical Sociology." *Journal of Applied Behavioral Science,* 1981, *17,* 347–350.

Bickman, L. "The Two Worlds of Evaluation: An Optimistic View of the Future." *Evaluation and Program Planning,* 1990, *13,* 421–422.

Brody, E. W. *Professional Practice Development: Meeting the Competitive Challenge.* New York: Praeger, 1989.

Brown, R. D., and Newman, D. L. "Ethical Principles and Evaluation Standards: Do They Match?" *Evaluation Review,* 1992, *16* (6), 650–663.

Canadian Evaluation Society Standards Development Committee. "Standards for Program Evaluation in Canada: A Discussion Paper." *Canadian Journal of Program Evaluation,* 1992, *7* (1), 157–170.

Caron, D. J. "Knowledge Required to Perform the Duties of an Evaluator." *Canadian Journal of Program Evaluation,* 1993, *8* (1), 59–78.

Comptroller General of the United States. *Government Auditing Standards.* Washington, D.C.: U.S. General Accounting Office, 1988.

Evaluation Research Society Standards Committee. "Evaluation Research Society Standards for Program Evaluation." In P. Rossi (ed.), *Standards for Evaluation Practice.* New Directions for Program Evaluation, no. 15. San Francisco: Jossey-Bass, 1982.

Hoffman, L. M. "Application of the Joint Committee Standards as Criteria for Evaluations in Louisiana." Paper presented at the annual meeting of the American Educational Research Association, New York, Mar. 1982.

House, E. R. *Professional Evaluation.* Newbury Park, Calif.: Sage, 1993.

Hurteau, M., and Trahan, M. *Review and Recommendations on the Elaboration of a Code of Ethics in the Search for a Professional Identity in Evaluation.* Ottawa: Canadian Evaluation Society, 1993.

Joint Committee on Standards for Educational Evaluation. *Standards for the Evaluation of Educational Programs, Projects, and Materials.* New York: McGraw-Hill, 1981.

Lincoln, Y. S. "The ERS Standards for Program Evaluation: Guidance for a Fledgling Profession." *Evaluation and Program Planning,* 1985, *8,* 251–253.

McKillip, J., and Garberg, R. "Demands of the Joint Committee's Standards for Educational Evaluation." *Evaluation and Program Planning,* 1986, *9,* 325–333.

Merwin, J. C., and Wiener, P. H. "Evaluation: A Profession?" *Educational Evaluation and Policy Analysis,* 1985, *7,* 253–259.

Moore, W. E. *The Professions: Roles and Rules.* New York: Russell Sage Foundation, 1970.

Morell, J. "Evaluation: Status of a Loose Coalition." *Evaluation Practice,* 1990, *11,* 213–219.

Office of the Comptroller General. *Working Standards for the Evaluation of Programs in Federal Departments and Agencies.* Ottawa, Canada: Supply and Services Canada, 1989.

Patton, M. Q. "The Challenge of Being a Profession." *Evaluation Practice,* 1990, *11,* 45–51.

Raven, J. "Some Limitations of the Standards." *Evaluation and Program Planning,* 1984, *7,* 363–370.

ARNOLD J. LOVE, an independent evaluation consultant based in Toronto, Canada, is currently serving a two-year term as president of the Canadian Evaluation Society.

The author views the main purpose of evaluation training programs as preparing practitioners. She suggests that evaluation training programs could consider the model provided by professional schools.

Alternative Models for the Structuring of Professional Preparation Programs

Jody L. Fitzpatrick

While we program evaluators appropriately spend much time actually conducting program evaluations and carrying out research or writing on program evaluation issues and problems, we spend comparatively little time considering how to educate evaluators. This problem is not unique to the field of evaluation. Given the reward structure of academia and the interests of faculty, most disciplines neglect broad issues concerning the structuring of curricula and development of teaching methods.

In program evaluation, our discussions of education have focused largely on descriptions of existing programs through survey research (May, Fleischer, Scheirer, and Cox, 1986), content analysis of syllabi (Conner and Davis, 1984; Sanders, 1986), or case studies (Cordray, Boruch, Howard, and Bootzin, 1986; Conner, 1986). Some authors have described trends in evaluation education (Altschuld and Thomas, 1991) or discussed methods used in particular courses (Brown and Dinnel, 1992; Preskill, 1992). Finally, some authors have concentrated on the competencies of evaluators. These competencies help to guide us in the development of programs (Anderson and Ball, 1978; Covert, 1992; Mertens, 1994).

This chapter explores issues concerning the structuring of programs for the educating of evaluators. By *structuring*, I mean the way in which programs should be organized and operated in order to achieve their desired aims. In considering the appropriate structuring of evaluation programs and alternative models for such structuring, I believe that we should apply our evaluation skills in much the same way that we do when we approach the evaluation of programs. Thus, to consider how evaluation programs should be structured, we should take a needs assessment or planning approach. These are some of

NEW DIRECTIONS FOR PROGRAM EVALUATION, no. 62, Summer 1994 © Jossey-Bass Publishers the questions that need to be answered: For what are our students being educated? What can we learn or adapt from other models of graduate education? What is the purpose of graduate education? How should we define *program evaluation* when we prepare evaluators? What are our students like, and how do their backgrounds influence the structure of our graduate programs? This chapter seeks to stimulate discussion and consideration of these broad issues so that evaluation programs can be planned in a more meaningful manner than they have been thus far.

For What Are Our Students Being Educated?

One way of approaching this question is to examine what graduates of evaluation programs tend to do when they have completed their graduate work. The limited published research in this area indicates that the majority of graduates at the master's and doctoral levels pursue work as practitioners (May, Fleischer, Scheirer, and Cox, 1986). The survey of evaluation programs by the authors just cited revealed that 50 percent of the recent doctoral graduates were working in applied settings, such as state government (18 percent), business and industry (17 percent), or private consulting (15 percent). Only 23 percent had found jobs in academe. Similarly, 53 percent of the graduates at the master's level were working in state or local agencies, and only 25 percent had gone on to doctoral study. A large proportion of both groups—71 percent of the doctoral graduates and 83 percent of the master's graduates—held positions in which evaluation was their primary responsibility. The fact that budgets in higher education are shrinking suggests that graduates will continue to pursue the practitioner rather than the academic role.

What are the implications of these placements for graduate education? First, those of us involved in the planning of graduate programs in evaluation must acknowledge our purpose as the training of practitioners. Since many academics come from traditional social science backgrounds that either devalue or ignore practitioner roles, we have tended to ignore the implications of the fact that we are training practitioners. Several of the case studies presented in an earlier *New Directions for Program Evaluation* sourcebook (Cordray, Boruch, Howard, and Bootzin, 1986; Wortman and Yeaton, 1986) illustrate this perspective. The former, who describe their program at Northwestern University, indicate that they "expect students to contribute to original research and to produce papers that are appropriate for submission to scholarly journals" (Cordray, Boruch, Howard, and Bootzin, 1986, p. 57). The latter focus on developing students who can be "intelligent consumers of research" (Wortman and Yeaton, 1986, p. 41). While academic evaluators should certainly strive to help evaluation accumulate knowledge of research issues by publishing articles in scholarly journals, such an objective may not be the most appropriate objective for the training of evaluators.

What Can We Learn from Other Models of Graduate Education?

It would be productive to look beyond the social science models of education to fields that have a greater focus on training practitioners. Professional schools provide such a model. Graduate education was traditionally identified as having a strong emphasis on the role of the student as an apprentice. Graduate students worked very closely with one professor who had only a handful of graduate students as his or her responsibility to educate. Today, when one of every twenty adults holds an advanced degree, numbers often prohibit such intimacy (Baird, 1990). However, many professional schools (nursing, medicine, social work) have managed to maintain a strong identification with the apprenticeship model. Law schools, which have long been criticized for inadequacies in this regard, are now developing clinical programs (Nyre and Reilly, 1979; Special Committee for a Study of Legal Education, 1980).

Professional schools also tend to be clearer than other graduate programs in articulating their goals and expectations for students while students are in the program. Baird (1990) contrasts programs in the arts and sciences, which are much less structured, more individualized, and more ambiguous in their demands on students, with the programs of professional schools, where curriculum tends to be relatively uniform across programs and expectations and steps toward graduation are relatively well standardized. Finally, professional goals for students after graduation are clearer than in traditional social science programs because of the practitioner focus. Scholars in the field of graduate education see such a model as less stressful and more productive for student learning than other graduate school models (Baird, 1969; Gutierrez, 1985).

Professional models certainly have their drawbacks, and we must use caution to ensure that we do not make the same mistakes when we adopt such models. For example, research on medical education indicates that the focus of medical school training has led many students away from general family practice toward specialization—a direction at odds with the needs of society (Broadhead, 1983; Sarickas and others, 1986). An analogy in the area of evaluation education is the heavy focus that some programs place on outcome studies and on designs and statistics. This focus often leads these programs to neglect monitoring or process studies and the methods and designs that are the most appropriate for them. Monitoring or process studies are often most useful for managers of new programs, as the evaluation literature now acknowledges. Nevertheless—perhaps because some academicians view such studies as less scholarly than the others—we slight them in our teaching and in our programs.

Using the professional school model forces us when we develop our curriculum to focus on the competencies required of practicing evaluators. Thus, our curriculum becomes not simply an incremental change from what we were taught in traditional social science graduate programs but a coherent program aimed at producing graduates who have the knowledge and skills needed to perform the kinds of evaluations that organizations need now and in the future. Barbara Gross Davis (1986) conceptualized these competencies in four broad skill areas: technical, conceptual, interpersonal and communication, and administrative. Comparing these competency areas to a content analysis of evaluation syllabi, James Sanders (1986, p. 18) noted: "What appears to be missing from the courses is an emphasis on the development of judgment and practical skills." The major topics that he lists also neglect the areas of interpersonal and communication and administrative skills. My experience in teaching students, managing evaluation staff, and conducting evaluations suggests that the value of the interpersonal and communication skills cannot be overemphasized. These are skills that practicing evaluators must have. Yet few courses in evaluation programs are devoted strictly to communication skills. Both course work and apprenticeship programs are needed to help students develop skills in this area.

The point about communication skills illustrates one aspect of the structure of evaluation programs that could be considered anew if we took a needs assessment approach to the development of a practitioner-oriented professional school model. While the literature on evaluator competencies is relatively extensive, such competencies must be based on studies of practitioners and users of evaluation if they are to serve as the foundation for a program. Studies should focus on describing what practitioners do; the types of communication, planning, administrative, and methodological skills required; and the needs that users of evaluation have of evaluators that evaluators are not currently meeting. Such research could be both national and local in scope. The information obtained from such studies could help faculty to plan a program consisting of courses and various types of concurrent apprenticeship efforts that could achieve the desired outcomes. Further study of successes and failures in other professional programs, such as the recent efforts in law schools for clinical placements, could facilitate the planning effort.

What Is the Purpose of Graduate Education?

While it is important for us to consider the future careers of our students when we plan programs, graduate education is more than simple job training. It is an induction into a profession. It serves the critical role of professional socialization. Bragg (1976, p. 6) defines the primary role of graduate school as one of "socialization to a particular role in society, the role of the professional. It is the acquisition of the specialized knowledge, skills, attitudes, values, norms, and interests of the profession that the individual wishes to practice. The end product of successful professional socialization is professional identity." Baird (1990) writes that such socialization, in particular the internalization of professional norms, enables society to permit people to perform in professions in a relatively autonomous manner without constant need for monitoring. The role of the student group and the role of faculty are among the primary methods for achieving such socialization.

Research on the effects of graduate school indicates that the student group can be an extremely effective socialization agent (Gregg, 1972; Konner, 1987). As graduate students develop group norms about their program and their chosen profession, the group effect helps students to assume their role as professionals. Similarly, the interaction among students helps to reinforce their interest in and commitment to their chosen field. Programs can be structured to enhance or impede these student effects. Programs that make extensive use of group projects stimulate the student interaction and cooperation that facilitate the desired student effects. Conversely, programs that concentrate on individualized instruction or foster competition among students reduce the productive effect that the student group can have. Group projects can be relatively easy to arrange in evaluation programs, and a group can often be more successful than an individual student in completing an evaluation project within the time constraints imposed by an academic term. In the case of evaluation projects, the use of student groups has some additional benefits: the insights that individual students can obtain from observing other students at work with users and from collaboration on issues ranging from the formulation of evaluation questions to the identification of appropriate methodologies and the ways of communicating results. The proliferation of small programs poses a danger for evaluation programs. Very small programs in evaluation that graduate only a few students each year may not have the critical mass needed to develop an effective student group whose primary interest is evaluation. These students may find their interests swamped by those of students committed to the department in which the evaluation program is housed, such as education, psychology, or sociology.

Faculty serve as another primary method of socialization for students. Unfortunately, there is little faculty-student contact. Forty percent of the graduate students surveyed by Craeger (1971) reported having had one or no informal contacts with their professors during the year, and 27 percent had no contact with any professor outside the classroom. Thus, we must consider methods for ensuring a relatively high level of faculty-student interaction outside the classroom when we structure evaluation programs.

To increase such contact, Wallach (1976) called for a return to the explicit apprenticeship model, in which a student works primarily with one professor, who serves as the student's role model. Such professors should have research, practitioner, and teaching skills if they are to serve effectively in such a mentor role. Such an apprenticeship model could be critical in developing the evaluative sensibility described by Davis (1986, p. 12): "Beyond skills and knowledge, an evaluative sensibility distinguishes professional excellence from mere adequacy. . . . Posing the critical question, discriminating between important and unimportant influences or events, spotting trends or issues, judging meaningful and practical significance, and recognizing the limits of evaluation—all are hallmarks of the accomplished professional." Such goals can be achieved only through intensive interaction with faculty in the practice of evaluation.

How can we foster such interaction? We need to make expectations clear to faculty and to students. New faculty must be counseled in appropriate ways of teaching and involving students in their work outside the classroom. Hiring decisions need to take candidates' aptitudes for performing such a role into account, and departments need to develop incentives that will encourage faculty to pursue this time-consuming and often unrewarded role. It needs to be mentioned that some faculty have found work with students rewarding in the sense that it has resulted in publications based on the students' work. A focus geared toward eventual publication in a scholarly journal defeats the purpose of training practitioners. It inculcates students with the values and norms of researchers, not of professional evaluators. Instead, we need to develop incentives that will encourage faculty to make apprenticing students in the professional evaluation role a primary focus and a reinforcer in its own right.

What Is a Program Evaluator?

For what other purposes are we educating our students? Another issue of concern is the content or substance of the goal. What is an evaluation practitioner? According to Worthen and Sanders (1991, p. 5), there is much agreement in the field that "evaluation is of necessity a multidimensional, pluralistic, situational, and political activity that encompasses much more than simple application of the skills of the empirical scientists." The difficulty lies in defining that *much more*. As with any new profession, program evaluation struggles to define its limits as a discipline. Public administration struggles with the same issues in defining its substance and then making use of that definition to determine its goals for the education of students (Ventriss, 1991; Henry, 1990).

John Crane (1988, p. 469) has referred to evaluation as a "public grazing area" for social scientists that has led evaluation to be defined by methodology. He, like others, sees a definition of program evaluation that focuses on methodology as inadequate for defining a disciplinary core. He argues that valuation rather than methodology should form the essence of program evaluation. William Foster (1991) has extended these issues of defining the discipline to the educating of students. He argues that both technical and moral training are needed in graduate education, but we have neglected the second in favor of the first. The moral training that he believes we should develop is "an ethics of participation and of inquiry" (Foster, 1991, p. 118). He makes a useful comparison to certain professional programs: "There is no systematic law-like knowledge base for training in social welfare, public, or educational administrators in professional, postgraduate educational programs, but this is not to dismiss the significance of such programs. Their significance lies largely in raising the consciousness of professionals about the nature of what it is they do and to develop within this community of practice the concept of agency. An agent is an active being with four dispositions: intelligence, curiosity, reflectiveness, and willfulness" (Foster, 1991, p. 119).

While Foster (1991) is writing about graduate programs in general, it is clear that his discussion is relevant to program evaluation. Acting as change agents, program evaluators can become active participants in the decision-making process. They can advocate for issues ranging from use of sound evaluation practices in decision making to the best way of meeting the needs of stakeholders. Educating students for such a role has many implications for program structure and curriculum.

In any case, the notion of evaluator as change agent and the focus on valuation merit discussion in the structuring of evaluation programs, because these notions help us to consider our purposes in educating practicing evaluators and socializing them to their profession. Such discussions may bring us back full circle to our studies of what evaluators actually do in the field. Do evaluators become involved as advocates, or would such a role discourage public administrators from the use of evaluation? What role does their advocacy take? Do they limit it largely to encouraging the use of evaluation methods that address public policy problems, or does it extend in some general way to advocacy of stakeholders' needs? Finally, given what evaluators actually do in the field, should educational programs develop goals that mirror current practice, or should programs develop goals that will use new definitions of the discipline to move toward changing the field?

Who Are Our Students and How Should Their Backgrounds Influence Our Programs?

The last area of concern for the planning of evaluation programs is the growing number of nontraditional students in graduate programs. Many graduate students today are not fresh from baccalaureate degrees and seeking additional education before beginning their professional careers. Instead, today's graduate students tend to be older, more experienced, and more mature than ever before (Korb, Schantz, and Zimbler, 1989). These students have life experiences either through other professional careers or occupations or through family and community responsibilities. These occupations and experiences mean that they approach graduate education with a perspective quite different from that of students just completing college. Their expectations, like their self-confidence, may often be much higher. Depending on their life circumstances, the work habits that they bring to the education environment may be more energetic, effective, and efficient than those of traditional students. Nontraditional students are often more serious in that they have explored other careers or life opportunities and in that their decision to change reflects a deliberate choice to pursue a career in program evaluation. Moreover, their exposure to many different life experiences and organizational settings prepares them to be sensitive to a variety of organizational cultures and to the differing needs and styles of the various stakeholders.

While these students bring advantages, they also present challenges. Returning students, particularly those with significant experience, dread the prospect of returning to school and of having their expertise and experiences denied. Balfour and Marini (1991, p. 482) write that "adults are often ambivalent about becoming involved in educational or training experiences because, although they want to continue learning, they expect they will be treated as though they lack the maturity, knowledge, and experience to contribute to the learning process." These authors discuss ways of structuring graduate education that allow students to become active participants in the process and that recognize their experience as a valuable resource. Their recommendations combine tenets of participative theories of management with philosophies and research on adult education. Such principles represent another critical component in our planning for the education of program evaluators.

Summary

In this chapter, I have reviewed several major issues with which I believe educators who plan and structure evaluation programs should be concerned. Rather than permitting our programs to develop incrementally, we should attempt to define our purposes. When we do so, we should take into account our goals for graduates, current practice in program evaluation, desired competencies and socialization, and the definition of evaluation itself. Having defined our purposes, we should then develop our programs. As we do, we should consider the results of research on graduate education, the roles of students and faculty, the place of the apprenticeship model, and the characteristics of our students. Consideration of these factors helps us to articulate the goals and philosophies of our programs. Only then can we consider courses, content, and competencies.

References

Anderson, S., and Ball, S. *The Profession and Practice of Program Evaluation*. San Francisco: Jossey-Bass, 1978.

Altschuld, J. W., and Thomas, P. M. "The Teaching of Evaluation: Twenty-Five Years of Growth and Change." *Theory into Practice*, 1991, *30*, 22–29.

Baird, L. L. "A Factor-Analytic Study of the Role of Graduate Students." *Journal of Educational Psychology*, 1969, *60*, 15–21.

Baird, L. L. "The Melancholy of Anatomy: The Personal and Professional Development of Graduate and Professional School Students." In J. A. Smart (ed.), *Higher Education: Handbook of Theory and Research*. Vol. 6. New York: Agathon Press, 1990.

Balfour, D. L., and Marini, F. "Child and Adult, X and Y: Reflections on the Process of Public Administration Education." *Public Administration Review*, 1991, *51*, 478–485.

Bragg, A. K. *The Socialization Process in Higher Education*. ERIC Higher Education Research Report, no. 7. Washington, D.C.: American Association of Higher Education, 1976.

Broadhead, R. *The Private Lives and Professional Identity of Medical Students*. New Brunswick, N.J.: Transaction Books, 1983.

Brown, R. D., and Dinnel, D. "Exploratory Studies of the Usefulness of a Developmental Approach for Supervising Evaluation Students." *Evaluation Review*, 1992, *17* (1), 23–39.

Conner, R. F., and Davis, B. G. "Analysis of Evaluation Courses." Paper presented at the meeting of the University of California Systemwide Evaluation Consortium, Berkeley, 1984.

Conner, R. F. "The Teaching of Evaluation in Interdisciplinary Programs: UC Irvine." In B. G. Davis (ed.), *Teaching of Evaluation Across the Disciplines*. New Directions for Program Evaluation, no. 29. San Francisco: Jossey-Bass, 1986.

Cordray, D., Boruch, R., Howard, K., and Bootzin, R. "The Teaching of Evaluation in Psychology: Northwestern University." In B. G. Davis (ed.), *Teaching of Evaluation Across the Disciplines*. New Directions for Program Evaluation, no. 29. San Francisco: Jossey-Bass, 1986.

Covert, R. W. "Successful Competencies in Preparing Professional Evaluators." Paper presented at the annual meeting of the American Evaluation Association, Seattle, Wash., 1992.

Craeger, J. A. *The American Graduate Student: A Normative Description*. Washington, D.C.: American Council on Education, 1971.

Crane, J. "Evaluation as Scientific Research." *Evaluation Review*, 1988, *12*, 467–482.

Davis, B. G. "Overview of the Teaching of Evaluation Across the Disciplines." In B. G. Davis (ed.), *Teaching of Evaluation Across the Disciplines*. New Directions for Program Evaluation, no. 29. San Francisco: Jossey-Bass, 1986.

Foster, W. "A Model of Agency for Postgraduate Education." In William G. Tierney (ed.), *Culture and Ideology in Higher Education*. New York: Praeger, 1991.

Gutierrez, F. J. "Counseling Law Students." *Journal of Counseling and Development*, 1985, *64*, 130–133.

Gregg, W. E. "Several Factors Affecting Graduate Student Satisfaction." *Journal of Higher Education*, 1972, *43*, 483–498.

Henry, N. "Root and Branch: Public Administration's Travail Toward the Future." In N. B. Lynn and A. Wildavsky (eds.), *Public Administration: The State of the Discipline*. Chatham, N.J.: Chatham House, 1990.

Konner, M. *Becoming a Doctor: A Journey of Initiation in Medical School*. New York: Viking Press, 1987.

Korb, R., Schantz, N., and Zimbler, L. *Student Financing of Graduate and Professional Education*. Washington, D.C.: National Center for Educational Statistics, Office of Educational Research and Improvement, U.S. Department of Education, 1989.

May, R. M., Fleischer, M., Scheirer, C. J., and Cox, G. B. "Directory of Evaluation Training Programs." In B. G. Davis (ed.), *Teaching of Evaluation Across the Disciplines*. New Directions for Program Evaluation, no. 29. San Francisco: Jossey-Bass, 1986.

Nyre, G. F., and Reilly, K. C. *Professional Education in the Eighties: Challenges and Responses*. AAHE-ERIC Research Report, no. 8. Washington, D.C.: American Association for Higher Education, 1979.

Preskill, H. "Students, Client, and Teacher: Observations from a Practicum in Evaluation." *Evaluation Practice*, 1992, *13*, 39–46.

Sanders, J. R. "The Teaching of Evaluation in Education." In B. G. Davis (ed.), *Teaching of Evaluation Across the Disciplines*. New Directions for Program Evaluation, no. 29. San Francisco: Jossey-Bass, 1986.

Sarickas, M. L., and others. "Difficulties Experienced by Medical Students in Choosing a Specialty." *Journal of Medical Education*, 1986, *61*, 467–469.

Special Committee for a Study of Legal Education. *Law Schools and Professional Education*. Chicago: American Bar Association, 1980.

Ventriss, C. "Contemporary Issues in American Public Administration Education: The Search for an Educational Focus." *Public Administration Review*, 1991, *51*, 4–14.

Wallach, M. A. "Psychology of Talent and Graduate Education." In S. M. Messick (ed.), *Individuality in Learning*. San Francisco: Jossey-Bass, 1976.

Worthen, B. R., and Sanders, J. R. "The Changing Face of Educational Evaluation." *Theory into Practice*, 1991, *30*, 3–12.

Wortman, P. M., and Yeaton, W. H. "The Teaching of Evaluation in Health Settings: University of Michigan." In B. G. Davis (ed.), *Teaching of Evaluation Across the Disciplines*. New Directions for Program Evaluation, no. 29. San Francisco: Jossey-Bass, 1986.

JODY L. FITZPATRICK is associate professor in the Graduate School of Public Affairs at the University of Colorado, Colorado Springs.

The single course continues to make a significant contribution to the evaluation field, but the nature of this contribution appears to have changed over time.

The Role of Single Evaluation Courses in Evaluation Training

Michael Morris

> A little learning is a dangerous thing; Drink deep, or taste not the Pierian spring.
>
> —Alexander Pope

> A little learning is not a dangerous thing to one who does not mistake it for a great deal.
>
> —William Allen White

It is White rather than Pope who serves as the inspiration for this chapter. The Pierian spring of evaluation knowledge need not and should not be limited only to those who have enrolled in one of the training programs described in Chapter Seven of this sourcebook. As a practical matter, of course, the issue is moot. Programs designed to prepare professional evaluators are far less numerous than the programs that do not have this purpose even if their curriculum includes an evaluation course. Indeed, it is likely that a significant proportion of the members of the American Evaluation Association (AEA) have their education roots in the second type of program. In 1992, for example, only 11 percent of the AEA's members listed evaluation as the area of their terminal degree ("Demographic Information," 1992). To be sure, many members whose degrees are in other fields (for example, education or psychology) probably specialized in evaluation in their graduate training and thus are the products of evaluation-focused programs. Nevertheless, there are a great many individuals—both inside and outside the AEA—whose formal exposure to evaluation during their graduate training consisted of a single course. What should be the goals of such a course? What competencies should students have when they emerge from it? How should the course be structured? This chapter addresses these and other questions.

The Single Course: Context and Design

In an important sense, the phrase *single course* can be a misnomer when we discuss evaluation training. It suggests an educational experience unrelated to the rest of a program's curriculum—something like an elective in eighteenth-century British literature on the worksheet of a student whose major was mechanical engineering. This is seldom the case when evaluation is concerned. The knowledge base for evaluation is closely linked to topics commonly covered in a variety of methodology and statistics courses found in graduate programs. Thus, a crucial contextual variable to consider is the extent to which a single evaluation course is embedded in a curriculum containing these complementary offerings. At one extreme would be a minimalist scenario, in which the evaluation course stood virtually alone, connected to little else in the program. At the other end of the continuum, one would find evaluation explicitly integrated into a sequence of several related courses.

Not surprisingly, these differing contexts are likely to have a significant relationship to the goals and instructional burdens associated with the single evaluation course. When the course is part of a network of offerings, it can deepen the coverage of the topics that are distinctive to evaluation (for example, models of evaluation, political concerns, issues of utilization), because the instructor can assume that students possess at least a rudimentary knowledge of such areas as the construction of questionnaires, the logic of experimentation, and data analysis. Where such a network is absent, it is usually necessary to devote some portion of the evaluation course—sometimes a large one—to the presentation of fundamentals of these basic topics. Consequently, those who emerge from the networked course will in general have been more thoroughly schooled in evaluation per se than those who exit the freestanding course. The implications of this difference are considerable, and I will address them later in this chapter.

The decisions that need to be made when we design the single evaluation offering involve more than the topics to be covered. For example, virtually everyone who has written about evaluation training has stressed the importance of incorporating real-world field experiences into the process (Anderson and Ball, 1978; Cronbach and others, 1980; Davis, 1986; Kelley and Jones, 1992; Morris, 1990, 1992; Preskill, 1992; Rossi and Freeman, 1993; Sechrest, 1980). There are several ways of accomplishing this purpose within the constraints imposed by the single-course format. One approach, which Conner (1986) has described in detail, consists of requiring each student to prepare an evaluation proposal for an ongoing program in an agency setting. In order to complete this task, students have to engage in many of the activities that are typically part of the entry and design phases of a full-fledged evaluation. The limitation of this procedure is that in the overwhelming majority of cases students do not have an opportunity to conduct the evaluations that they have proposed.

At first glance, one might view apprenticeships (Cronbach and others, 1980; Quill, 1992) as a solution to the limitations associated with the proposal-only strategy. In apprenticeships, students help experienced evaluators to carry out one or more phases of an actual evaluation that the evaluator is conducting. Unfortunately, it is rare that such an arrangement can accommodate more than just a few of those enrolled in the type of evaluation course discussed in this chapter. For one thing, there are often not enough practicing evaluators based in the educational setting that offers the course (or in other settings accessible to students) to meet the apprenticeship needs during the semester in question. More important, the apprenticeship model is geared toward those who plan to specialize in the art in which they are apprenticing. In contrast, the hallmark of the single-course scenario is that students are not being trained as professional evaluators. Thus, they are usually not in a position to extend their participation in an evaluation project significantly beyond one semester, as apprenticeships often require.

A third approach is to use field projects in which teams of students are responsible for conducting an entire evaluation from start to finish during the course. Although some authors have expressed doubts about the feasibility of achieving such a goal (Conner, 1986; Weeks, 1982; Wortman, Cordray, and Reis, 1980), there is clear evidence that this strategy can be successful under certain circumstances (Morris, 1992). Foremost among them is a commitment to small-scale projects, that is, to evaluations that one can reasonably expect to be completed within a semester. Evaluations that fall into this category are usually relatively basic in terms of the methodological and statistical demands that they place upon students, and they tend to emphasize simplified needs assessments, program monitoring, and short-term impact studies rather than sophisticated outcome analyses or cost-benefit or cost-effectiveness investigations. Another important ingredient in this model is strict deadlines, which the instructor must enforce, for such tasks as submitting proposals and final reports to the evaluation client.

Overall, the start-to-finish approach gives students more exposure to all the stages of an evaluation than the proposal-only approach. It is also easier to implement in practice than the apprenticeship model, especially if the instructor can solicit and screen a list of potential evaluation projects before the course begins (Morris, 1992).

In some instances, the single evaluation course may not be able to provide students with any field experiences. In such cases, instructors could consider using a simulation to address issues that real evaluations typically encounter (Mertens, 1989; Morris, 1981; Willer, Bartlett, and Northman, 1978). Simulations in which the instructor provides students with data sets (genuine or

manufactured) to analyze for the purposes of preparing a final report are especially valuable (Boruch and Reis, 1980). Indeed, the high degree of control that
instructors can exercise over the dynamics of a simulation can tempt them to
employ this technique even when real-life field projects are available. As a general rule, the temptation should be resisted. No matter how well a simulation
is designed, it will almost always lack the subtle nuances and challenges, especially of a process and interpersonal nature, that an actual evaluation project
faces on a day-to-day basis.

What Emerges from the Single Evaluation Course?

If the title of this section evokes an unsettling image of semiconscious crea-
tures marching stiff legged out of Doctor Frankenstein's laboratory, such an
image is probably an accurate reflection of the concerns of many evaluators
about the competencies that graduates of the single-course experience will possess (Sanders, 1986). However, as the preceding discussion should have made
evident, the nature of single courses can vary greatly from one setting to
another. For example, the skill level produced by a freestanding course that
has no fieldwork component is likely to be quite different from the skill level
produced by a highly networked course that requires a start-to-finish evaluation project. Although there are undoubtedly many intermediate points
between these extremes, for heuristic purposes it is helpful to view the degree
of competence that students achieve in dichotomous terms. Accordingly, I will
use the expressions *educated consumer* (EC) and *household handyman* (HH) to
characterize the lower and higher skill levels, respectively, that various forms
of the single course can develop.

The Educated Consumer. Because the single-course experience of the
educated consumers occurs near the freestanding/no-field-project end of the
continuum, the ECs do not typically possess the level of skill required to conduct an evaluation without supervision. However, they can articulate meaningful evaluation questions at a general level and develop evaluation designs
and data collection strategies for the programs that they fund, administer, or
staff. Thus, they should be able to interact effectively with those who actually
evaluate these programs, and in this sense they can be knowledgeable, moti-
vated consumers of professional evaluation services.

ECs can distinguish a high-quality evaluation from a low-quality one, and
they can participate in the evaluation process in a way that helps to produce a
high-quality outcome. For example, they are sensitive to the major issues
raised by the professional standards that have been advanced for the field (ERS
Standards Committee, 1982; Joint Committee on Standards for Educational
Evaluation, 1981), and, within the limits imposed by their technical expertise,
they can recognize when these standards are being observed or violated. It is
also possible for ECs to serve as nonprofessional evaluation resources to other

staff within their organization—for example, by helping them to conceptualize the evaluation challenges associated with their programs.

The fact that ECs do not have the expertise needed to conduct evaluations on their own should not cause us to minimize the importance of this role. Experienced evaluators are all too familiar with the frustrations of working with administrators, staff, and other constituencies who have little or no understanding of evaluation. The quality of an evaluation conducted under such circumstances can be severely compromised, sometimes to the point where it becomes virtually worthless. This is less likely to happen with ECs. Rather than objecting to sound evaluation practice, they are inclined to insist on it or at least to support it. Thus, just as an athlete's performance tends to rise or fall in response to the skill level of his or her competitors, the quality of an evaluation in part reflects the sophistication of the major participants in the process who are not evaluators.

The Household Handyman. The household handyman is customarily thought of as someone who can do some repairs around his or her home. Complex jobs requiring sophisticated tools are usually out of the question, and you usually would not pay such a person to come into your own home to do these repairs. Household handyman seems to be an apt metaphor for students whose single evaluation course falls near the highly networked/full-field-project end of the spectrum. They are likely to have the competencies required to conduct certain types of evaluations of certain types of programs within their own organization. For example, needs assessments and process or implementation evaluations can vary greatly in the demands placed on an evaluator's technical expertise. Situations in which these demands are relatively modest are probably good candidates for involvement by an HH. Experimental and quasi-experimental outcome studies of limited scope are also possible, especially if strong methodology and statistics courses are part of the individual's background. However, cost-benefit and cost-effectiveness analyses are typically beyond the HH's reach except in cases where his or her graduate training has included a nontrivial dose of economics.

Not surprisingly, HHs are better equipped than ECs to serve as internal consultants on evaluation issues to their agency colleagues. This means that they can provide more specific advice and guidance than ECs can. Overall, having a combination of HHs and ECs in key positions within an organization helps to create a climate that is supportive of well-designed evaluations and that in some ways resembles a miniaturized version of Campbell's (1969, 1971) experimental society.

Implications

Altschuld and Thomas (1991) describe the critical role that single courses played in evaluation training during the field's formative years. Against the background of the issues considered in this chapter, it would appear that a strong case can be made that single courses continue to contribute in significant ways to evaluation training, although not directly in the preparation of professional evaluators. Rather, they help to establish programmatic environments that are conducive to successful evaluations and that in many cases provide individuals with the skills necessary to undertake modest evaluative efforts on their own.

When the limitations of the single-course format are viewed from this perspective, they assume less threatening proportions. It is certainly true, as Sanders (1986, p. 23) maintains, that "the development of competence in evaluation requires much more than a one-semester course." However, to the extent to which one views competence as something other than all-or-nothing, it is possible to acknowledge the range of skills produced by various configurations of the single-course model. It should also be noted that this model lays the foundation for more focused, postgraduate evaluation training (for example, in intensive workshops and summer institutes) that can enhance skill levels to the point where a household handyman becomes a self-made evaluator. Indeed, in some instances individuals may even progress to the point of being indistinguishable in their evaluation competence from graduates of programs designed to train professional evaluators.

Graduate programs define their goals for the single-course experience explicitly, especially in view of the fact that the HH model requires linkages between courses that the EC approach does not call for. Moreover, it is questionable whether one section of the course can do justice to both models at once. Thus, combining ECs and HHs in the same class is likely to be frustrating for both groups, jokes about physics for poetry majors aside.

Beyond the observation that courses intended for HHs should provide more in-depth coverage of evaluation topics than courses designed for ECs, specific recommendations for the content of single courses are unnecessary and perhaps even ill advised. Evaluation training continues to be discipline based for the most part, and each discipline tends to stress the aspects of evaluation that have the greatest relevance for its self-perceived needs. Hence, suggestions that would be quite reasonable for an introduction-to-program-evaluation course based in a psychology department could very well be out of place for the introductory course that an education department would offer.

Virtually no systematic data on the topics that evaluation courses cover have been gathered, but Davis (1986) is probably close to the mark when she identifies four broad areas of emphasis in evaluation curricula: the historical background of evaluation, models of evaluation, techniques and methods, and issues in the practice of evaluation (for example, political, social, and ethical concerns). Each of these areas gives instructors a great deal of territory in which to roam when they select the particular issues on which they will focus in their individual courses. When we consider the relative youth of evaluation as a field of inquiry and practice, this level of freedom seems appropriate.

Discussions of the role of the single course in evaluation training would benefit tremendously from research on the evaluation activities in which students engaged after they graduated from the program in which they had taken the course. What percentage actually end up conducting evaluations in their work settings? What types of evaluations do they conduct? How many assume roles close to that of the educated consumer in which they regularly or occasionally interact with professional evaluators? To what extent do graduates of the single-course experience pursue additional training in evaluation? Do any self-made evaluators eventually emerge? What impact if any does the nature of the student's graduate program (for example, master's or doctoral, education or psychology) have on these outcomes? And, perhaps most important, what would these graduates want to tell those of us who are responsible for training about course content and curriculum structure?

Admittedly, it will not be easy to gather this information. Given that most programs find it difficult enough to obtain follow-up data on graduates' activities in the areas for which they have specifically been trained, it would certainly be understandable if the motivation of program coordinators to gather data on additional, tangential activities was low. Even so, once the decision to track program graduates longitudinally has been made (Hoffnung, Morris, and Jex, 1986), the extra effort involved in collecting this information is probably minimal in objective if not subjective terms. Indeed, if there is any field that should be well equipped to handle the challenges involved in conducting research on its outcomes, it is evaluation.

Conclusion

A comprehensive approach to the conceptualizing of evaluation training should certainly address the role of the single evaluation course. Thus, it is very encouraging that the editors of this volume have elected to include a chapter on this subject. Although a little knowledge can be a dangerous thing, program evaluation is a field in which total ignorance is much worse. Evaluation is most likely to achieve its dual goals of demonstrating scientific credibility and bettering the human condition in an environment where it is not just the professional evaluation community that has access to relevant knowledge and skills. To the extent to which the single course can help to produce such an environment, it will play a major role in fulfilling the potential for empowerment that is inherent in evaluation.

References

Altschuld, J. W., and Thomas, P. M. "The Teaching of Evaluation: Twenty-Five Years of Growth and Change." *Theory Into Practice*, 1991, 30 (1), 22–29.
Anderson, S. B., and Ball, S. *The Profession and Practice of Program Evaluation.* San Francisco: Jossey-Bass, 1978.

Boruch, R. F., and Reis, J. "The Student, Evaluative Data, and Secondary Analysis." In L. Sechrest (ed.), *Training Program Evaluators*. New Directions for Program Evaluation, no. 8. San Francisco: Jossey-Bass, 1980.

Campbell, D. T. "Reforms as Experiments." *American Psychologist,* 1969, *24*, 409–429.

Campbell, D. T. "Methods for the Experimenting Society." Paper presented at the annual meeting of the American Psychological Association, Washington, D.C., August 1971.

Conner, R. "The Teaching of Evaluation in Interdisciplinary Programs: UC Irvine." In B. G. Davis (ed.), *Teaching of Evaluation Across the Disciplines*. New Directions for Program Evaluation, no. 29. San Francisco: Jossey-Bass, 1986.

Cronbach, L. J., Ambron, S. R., Dornbusch, S. M., Hess, R. D., Hornick, R. C., Phillips D. C., Walker, D. F., and Weiner, S. S. *Toward Reform of Program Evaluation: Aims, Methods, and Institutional Arrangements*. San Francisco: Jossey-Bass, 1980.

Davis, B. G. (ed.). *Teaching of Evaluation Across the Disciplines*. New Directions for Program Evaluation, no. 29. San Francisco: Jossey-Bass, 1986.

Davis, B. G. "Overview of the Teaching of Evaluation Across the Disciplines." In B. G. Davis (ed.), *Teaching of Evaluation Across the Disciplines*. New Directions for Program Evaluation, no. 29. San Francisco: Jossey-Bass, 1986.

"Demographic Information on AEA Members." *Evaluation Practice News,* October 1992, pp. 5–7.

ERS Standards Committee. "Evaluation Research Society Standards for Program Evaluation." In P. H. Rossi (ed.), *Standards for Evaluation Practice*. New Directions for Program Evaluation, no. 15. San Francisco: Jossey-Bass, 1982.

Hoffnung, R. J., Morris, M., and Jex, S. "Training Community Psychologists at the Master's Level: A Case Study of Outcomes." *American Journal of Community Psychology,* 1986, *14*, 339–349.

Joint Committee on Standards for Educational Evaluation. *Standards for Evaluations of Educational Programs, Projects, and Materials*. New York: McGraw-Hill, 1981.

Kelley, J. M., and Jones, B. J. "Teaching Evaluation by Doing It: A Multiple-Utility Approach." *Evaluation and Program Planning,* 1992, *15*, 55–59.

Mertens, D. M. (ed.). *Creative Ideas For Teaching Evaluation*. Boston: Kluwer Academic Publishers, 1989.

Morris, M. "Teaching Evaluation Research via a Semester-Long Simulation." Paper presented at the annual meeting of the American Psychological Association, Los Angeles, August 1981.

Morris, M. "A Nightmare in Elm City: When Evaluation Field Experiences Meet Organizational Politics." *Evaluation Review,* 1990, *14*, 91–99.

Morris, M. "Field Experiences in Evaluation Courses: Increasing Their Value to Students and Sponsors." *Evaluation and Program Planning,* 1992, *15*, 61–66.

Preskill, H. "Students, Client, and Teacher: Observations from a Practicum in Evaluation." *Evaluation Practice,* 1992, *13*, 39–46.

Quill, J. "Using Consultants in Evaluation Research: A Client's Perspective." *Evaluation and Program Planning,* 1992, *15*, 67–69.

Rossi, P.H., and Freeman, H. E. *Evaluation: A Systematic Approach*. (5th ed.) Newbury Park, Calif.: Sage, 1993.

Sanders, J. R. "The Teaching of Evaluation in Education." In B. G. Davis (ed.), *Teaching of Evaluation Across the Disciplines*. New Directions for Program Evaluation, no. 29. San Francisco: Jossey-Bass, 1986.

Secrest, L. (ed.). *Training Program Evaluators*. New Directions for Program Evaluation, no. 8. San Francisco: Jossey-Bass, 1980.

Weeks, E. C. "The Value of Experimental Approaches to Evaluation Training." *Evaluation and Program Planning,* 1982, *5*, 21–30.

Willer, B. S., Bartlett, D. P., and Northman, F. E. "Simulation as a Method for Teaching Program Evaluation." *Evaluation and Program Planning,* 1978, *1*, 221–228.

Wortman, P. M., Cordray, D. S., and Reis, J. "Training for Evaluation Research: Some Issues." In L. Sechrest (ed.), *Training Program Evaluators*. New Directions for Program Evaluation, no. 8. San Francisco: Jossey-Bass, 1980.

MICHAEL MORRIS is professor of psychology at the University of New Haven, where he serves as director of graduate field training in community psychology.

*In 1988, the U.S. General Accounting Office started an ongoing,
comprehensive evaluation training program for its staff. This
chapter sketches the program and describes the major substantive
areas of its curriculum.*

Evaluator Training in a Government Setting

Nancy Kingsbury, Terry E. Hedrick

The U.S. General Accounting Office (GAO) is a nonpartisan agency in the legislative branch of the federal government. Its statutory mission, established by the Budget and Accounting Act of 1921, is (among other things) to "investigate, at the seat of government or elsewhere, all matters relating to the receipt, disbursement, and application of public funds" (Budget and Accounting Act, 1921). Over the years, this responsibility has evolved from detailed audits of individual agency purchases into economy and efficiency reviews of government programs and more recently to a wide-ranging array of program evaluations and policy analyses. With very few exceptions, any program or activity funded with federal tax dollars can be the subject of a GAO review. And as Congress grapples with the difficult decisions of the 1990s, the issues that the GAO is asked to evaluate mirror the breadth and complexity of the day's headlines. A recent sample of study requests includes these questions: What strategies have been most effective in reaching hard-to-serve recipients of welfare programs? What factors drive health care costs? How feasible are various approaches to the development of geothermal energy? Are federal plans for the elimination of tuberculosis from the United States achievable? What are the causes and effects of the European currency crisis? What is the best strategy for response by the federal government to natural disasters? Can nonnuclear designs for aircraft carriers and submarines meet the Navy's need for future missions? What interventions are necessary to end the underrepresentation of women and minorities in federal agencies?

In September 1993, the GAO had about 4,900 staff. Three-quarters were engaged in evaluation and auditing work. Evaluators are organized into thirty-six issue areas that correspond roughly to government programmatic areas, such as health policy, employment and training, environmental issues, tax policy and administration, administration of justice, management of defense and space programs, international trade, and federal management issues.

Because a substantial part of the GAO's evaluation work is carried out on site where government programs operate, evaluation staff are located in Washington, D.C., in fourteen regional offices around the U.S. continent, and in two overseas offices (one in Hawaii, the other in Germany). Like many federal agencies, the GAO expects to reduce its size over the next few years, although there is little likelihood that the work that it will be asked to do will decrease. Accordingly, the GAO is investing significantly in technology improvements (computer networks, videoconferencing) that can improve its productivity and in improving its work processes through total quality management (TQM).

Evaluation and Evaluators at the GAO

The GAO defines *evaluation* broadly. The term is used to describe a range of activities. Depending on the context, it can be synonymous with *audit, review,* or *policy analysis.* Methodologies and techniques from a variety of disciplines are often brought to bear on an assignment, and, because of the agency's history in the accounting tradition, the results of the work must meet traditional government auditing and accounting standards as well as the standards of other professional disciplines.

Most staff responsible for carrying out reviews of government programs are called *evaluators,* and they are expected to demonstrate strong generic skills in project planning, data gathering and analysis, written and oral communication, and interpersonal communications and management areas. However, they also need specialized expertise.

The GAO recruits staff from an array of the professional disciplines found in colleges and universities throughout the country. In the 1950s and 1960s, the GAO recruited almost exclusively from the accounting profession. In recent years, it has greatly diversified its hiring practices, hiring master's degree and doctoral level graduates in economics, the social sciences, public policy, public administration, and business administration. It continues to recruit accountants but generally at the bachelor's level. Increasingly, GAO staff are maintaining their professional identities (for example, as an economist) after entering the agency. Nevertheless, the requirements of the work necessitate that members of each discipline become familiar with the terminology and methods of other disciplines.

Although disciplinary diversity is clearly an important part of the GAO's institutional capability, it is equally important that there be a common set of core values and working procedures that overlay the variety of disciplinary perspectives. It is essential to have a common understanding of the GAO's mission, of what is meant by the expression "quality work," of the GAO's expectations for the way in which work will be carried out, of the way in which the executive and legislative branches operate and intersect, and of the way in which the GAO will ultimately meet the information needs of Congress and provide value to the taxpayer. Meeting all these needs while developing specific technical and computer skills poses a large challenge for the GAO's training programs. Training serves as a vehicle for establishing values, teaching agency procedures, and understanding the broad context of evaluation work.

Training at the GAO

In 1988, the GAO established its own Training Institute. Training and education responsibilities were consolidated and separated from career counseling, personnel, and organizational development support. The intent was to highlight the importance that the agency places on training and professional development. Investing in staff development was deemed critical to meeting the information needs of Congress.

In comparison with other federal agencies, the GAO makes a relatively large investment in training opportunities for its staff. The physical plant includes two major training centers in Washington, D.C., that have a total of seventeen classrooms. Each regional office also has space and equipment for training activities. Completion of a nationwide videoconferencing capability this year will permit training to be provided simultaneously in headquarters and regional offices.

GAO evaluators averaged seventy-four hours of continuing education in 1992. Two-thirds of that training was delivered by the Training Institute. The institute has a roster of 210 active courses and offers more than a thousand classes a year (Training Institute. . ., 1991). Evaluators have also been given significant resources, both centrally and within organizational units, to participate in professional development activities outside the GAO. The agency's origin in accounting contributes directly to this emphasis on training by imposing a continuing education requirement on all evaluators. To continue to be deemed qualified to do the GAO's audit and evaluation work, every evaluator must obtain a minimum eighty hours of training every two years.

Teaching Evaluation in a Work Setting

The environment of the GAO makes demands and imposes constraints on the design of training programs that are quite different from the forces that operate in academic settings. Our students are adults ranging from recent graduates of graduate-level programs to experienced evaluators who have broad evaluation and management experiences and mature auditors nearing retirement. Almost all these students work full-time and expect training to be directly relevant to what they will do on the job the very next week.

Work schedules and geographic dispersion require that training be delivered in intensive segments. A typical Training Institute course consists of two to four successive eight-hour days of training. This pattern permits a short period of full-time training (about all that is manageable given the press of ongoing work), and it gives regional participants reasonable travel time. This concentrated, full-time training schedule and the nature and expectations of the Training Institute's students—evaluator staff—heavily influence training methods. Most courses are a mixture of lecture, case studies, and opportunities for practical application of skills through role playing or demonstration, and most courses make extensive use of materials taken directly from GAO work. When possible, we give training participants opportunities to use material from their current assignments in class exercises (for example, by using real data from an ongoing assignment when they practice writing testimony).

In part as a means of focusing training on skills and activities directly related to the work, instructors are heavily drawn from line staff and managers. Many of our senior executives regularly act as course instructors. This pattern of training delivery requires development of course frameworks and instructional materials that are easy for multiple instructors to use. We also train our instructors to teach effectively. We are more likely to use external than internal instructors for courses in such things as statistics, writing, computer software, and generic management topics.

Major Areas of Emphasis

Overall, the GAO's formal training program for evaluators has six areas of emphasis: agency mission and policies, assignment planning and execution, communication skills and strategies, computers and information technology, workplace relations and management, and issue area expertise. With the exception of issue area training, the courses in each area have been designated as required, core, or elective and determined to be appropriate for staff, senior staff, management, and/or executive levels.

All evaluators must take the required courses, which contain information that the agency believes is necessary for all persons regardless of prior education or work experience. Core courses contain material with which all evaluators should be familiar, but the agency recognizes that individuals may excuse themselves from specific courses if they have previously mastered the material. Elective courses can be selected to fill specific needs, depending on the type of work in which the individual is currently engaged. Courses at the staff and senior staff levels are concentrated in technical areas. Courses at the management and executive levels emphasize management. The training provided for the upper levels often relies on external opportunities for continuing education, such as professional conferences. Evaluators move through a structured set of courses as they progress in their careers.

The GAO's curriculum structure was developed in collaboration with an advisory committee of managers drawn from the agency's divisions and offices.

Specific courses have been developed over the past four years, and only in the past year can the GAO be said to have fully implemented its evaluator curriculum. The six sections that follow describe each of the major substantive areas.

Mission, Policies, and Individual Responsibilities. All new staff members are required to attend an initial orientation course that describes the GAO's history, its mission, its role in supporting congressional decision making, ethics guidelines, and the policies and procedures for the conduct of evaluation assignments. Subsequent required courses that evaluators take in the next few years elaborate on standards for work, internal control issues concerning the quality of acceptable evidence, and processes for ensuring accuracy in the agency's reports.

As staff move up the career ladder after each promotion, they are invited to attend so-called promotion programs that lay out the organization's expectations for their new roles. The discussions in these programs are structured both around people issues—interpersonal communication, supervision, performance feedback—and around planning and reporting issues—for example, what it means to have responsibility for directing an evaluation or managing the work of multiple teams of evaluators. At mid levels, these programs can include special topics, such as information on a manager's equal employment opportunity responsibilities.

Assignment Planning and Execution. Each audit or evaluation at the GAO is referred to as an *assignment,* and the skills necessary to design and manage an assignment are a crucial part of the GAO's internal training program for newly hired evaluators. The goal here is twofold: to create an awareness of other professional disciplines and to build specific skills.

The overall intent of this part of the curriculum is to foster an awareness of the wide range of work that the agency does and of the need to apply appropriate methodologies when the work is done. All entering staff are required to attend a workshop on the selection of an approach and methodology. The workshop provides guidance on how to take an area of congressional concern and develop focused questions that can be answered within the constraints imposed by resources and time. Workshop participants then analyze these questions to determine how they can most appropriately be answered. Staff then take core methods courses on compliance auditing, economy and efficiency reviews, program evaluation, and policy analysis. Follow-on courses on such topics as procurement and contract processes, financial management, budgeting processes, fraud awareness, and special issues in economics are available. The goals are for all individuals—staff and managers—to become comfortable with a variety of types of work and to be able to work effectively in a multidisciplinary environment.

To meet the skill-building goal, the institute offers courses on such topics as sampling, questionnaire design and structured interviewing, applied statistics (basic classes and elective classes on advanced topics, such as log-linear modeling and time series analysis), and qualitative methods. At entry, staff are provided with self-paced training materials on organizing their documentation (work papers) for the evidence and analysis that support an audit or evaluation.

Communication. Although a GAO evaluation team may conduct an excellent study, the value of the study will be weakened significantly if it is not communicated effectively in published reports and oral briefings. For this reason, the GAO's curriculum gives evaluators a series of courses reflecting the latest research on written and oral communication and on cognitive psychology. For example, instructors may discuss readability principles and factors that increase the retention of information read.

Writing courses at the entry level clarify the GAO's basic communications policy and differentiate between academic writing and workplace writing. The focus is on producing an institutional—not an individual—product. In class, evaluators work on skills that they need in order to write GAO documents—for example, analyzing the writing situation, writing collaboratively, recognizing the difference between writer-based and reader-based documents, assessing the readability of their own documents, and using review comments to improve documents.

Class exercises for senior staff show how writing and thinking are inextricably linked and how the structure of a written report can affect its interpretation. Training participants also practice constructing a succinct message out of masses of data. Using data from a case study, evaluators develop report issues, prepare for a message conference (a meeting in which all evaluation team members, advisers, and managers discuss the evaluation results and agree on their interpretation), and conduct a simulated message conference. Message conferences are stressed because they improve the quality and timeliness of the documents produced and reduce unnecessary rework. A course for managers called Managing Writing reviews the writing principles embodied in the curriculum, suggests strategies for managing the writing process, and presents ideas about the role of oral and written communication in public policy processes.

The writing curriculum also includes specialized courses that help staff to write specific kinds of documents, such as an executive summary or written testimony for oral presentation. These two kinds of writing are emphasized because both are highly visible statements of the GAO's work. Both kinds of written summaries receive close scrutiny, and many readers may never read the full evaluation report. During the testimony course, evaluators develop testimony by following guidelines for effective congressional presentations. They practice testimony-writing skills and receive constructive feedback. The course also includes discussions with executives who excel in the delivery of written testimony.

Oral communication is equally important, because much of the agency's work is conveyed through briefings and testimony. Training on oral presentation skills begins during the first three months after a new evaluator starts work, and it seeks to improve his or her interviewing and briefing skills. The follow-on course is dedicated to honing presentation skills; it makes use of videotaping and feedback. Electives are available at a more advanced level to improve presentation skills and learn how to conduct meetings effectively. At the most advanced levels, managers and executives can take hands-on courses involving practice in communicating effectively with the media and delivering oral testimony to Congress. Figure 6.1 shows how the content of the communications courses varies by position.

Computer Use. As a large organization, the GAO uses several software packages that must be supported with technical assistance and training. Several years of experience have taught us that users prefer that course material delivered in the classroom be very brief. Material is often delivered in modules—for example, WordPerfect sort features, WordPerfect text columns, Lotus 1-2-3 data tables. Users can enroll in the course most suited to their immediate needs. Forty courses are available (Training Institute. . ., 1991). They relate to word processing applications, spreadsheets, and database management systems. Additional training is available on microcomputers; data analysis packages, such as SAS and SPSS; computer communications; and support for local area networks. As the agency is moving to design and implement software applications for organizing, sharing, and accessing working papers and databases, the institute is designing training to support their use. Steps are also being taken to revise existing training in ways that recognize how these applications and the use of local area networks can change the ways in which work gets done.

Figure 6.1. Communications Courses in the GAO's Evaluator Curricu-

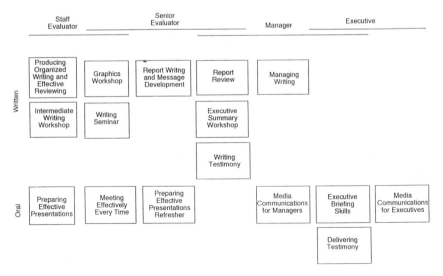

Note: Introductory Evaluator Training, the two-week orientation, includes modules on writing and oral briefing skills.

Workplace Relations and Management. Training in the area of workplace relations and management contains material that traditionally has been classified as both soft and hard skills. As one might expect, the institute offers classes on time management, relations with Congress, and management of one's issue area, that is, a body of work in an area like transportation or energy. These kinds of courses focus on planning and coordination processes. Supervision and performance management seminars are also available.

Courses on interpersonal relations in the workplace, mediation, diversity in the workplace, and advanced communications and negotiations are newer additions to the GAO's curriculum. As the GAO has become increasingly involved with total quality management (TQM), the emphasis on interpersonal communication, teamwork, and management skills has increased. Recent hires have an opportunity to enroll in such courses as Workplace Relations and Communications. Mid-level managers take Managing Quality Improvement, and top-level executives learn about the role and responsibilities of quality councils. Five-day courses prepare leaders of problem-solving teams to use appropriate tools and techniques, teach fellow team members, and be aware of how to foster positive group dynamics. Additional training is expected to be added in this area as the GAO advances in its implementation of TQM.

This area also contains courses to build skills and heighten awareness and knowledge about key supervisory and management responsibilities. All supervisory staff recently participated in workshops on ways of preventing sexual harassment in the work environment, and a similar course is now available to nonsupervisory staff. All supervisors and managers have already received training on their equal employment opportunity (EEO) responsibilities. To maintain this awareness, the GAO automatically enrolls newly promoted staff in the EEO workshop. And in recognition of the increasing diversity of its work force and of the need to have a work environment that makes all staff feel welcome and valued, the institute has started to provide workshops on the valuing of diversity.

Issue Area Training. As noted earlier, the GAO has thirty-six issue areas covering work in areas as wide-ranging as national security policy and national resource management. Generally, the Training Institute has neither the expertise nor the resources needed to develop issue area subject matter training, so in most cases issue area groups pursue their own strategies to develop and maintain staff proficiency. These strategies can include inviting subject matter experts to give informal talks, using consultants on specific projects, and holding planning conferences with invited participants from government agencies and academic and other relevant groups, including businesses, professional associations, and think tanks.

However, major training initiatives have been supported internally in two key issue areas. In the financial management area, the institute worked closely with the GAO's accounting and financial management experts to develop a financial auditing curriculum. And in the information management technology area, the institute has offered courses on such topics as computer security, telecommunications, and systems development. Several master's-level courses leading to a certificate in information systems from the George Washington University have been offered at the GAO's training center on a regular basis at the end of the workday.

Self-Paced Training

Besides classroom courses, the institute provides a variety of self-paced courses in interactive multimedia, audio, video, and print formats. Many of these course offerings are related to computer software packages, but others cover such topics as management and supervision, human resource management, writing, and administrative support activities. In most cases, courses can be mailed to the work site and used on the individual's own computer. When special equipment is needed or licensing restrictions make widespread distribution impractical, individuals can sign up to take such courses in the institute's learning center. Acceptance of this type of course delivery has grown: Self-paced hours increased by two-thirds in the past year. More than 1,300 evaluators enrolled in self-paced courses in fiscal year 1993, and there have been about 800 course completions to date.

Lessons Learned

Developing and delivering the GAO's evaluator curriculum has been a continuous learning process for everyone involved. Several valuable lessons have been learned that may be useful to others who have a responsibility for training functions in similar contexts.

First, job relevance is critical. Course developers and instructors need to be able to assess training needs accurately, design effective learning experiences, and demonstrate to training participants that the training material is directly relevant to their work. Training is not an end in itself; it must be designed to support the effectiveness of the individual and the organization. One technique for enhancing the relevance of training is to design courses that use real case studies or have the students bring ongoing work to class and apply the material to it. This means that instructors have to be adaptable and quite proficient in their area of expertise.

Second, the involvement of line managers and staff increases the credibility and quality of training. The GAO's curriculum was developed under the guidance of a management advisory committee, and all decisions regarding mandated, core, and elective courses were made by this committee. Housing decision-making authority in the "line" makes ownership of the curriculum greater than if the training department were to make all the decisions. Executives, managers, and senior staff also often serve as instructors or presenters on panels or contribute course material, thereby endorsing the value of training and building commitment.

Third, training needs to deliver consistent messages at all levels. The GAO's curriculum structure was intended to be an integrated one, with similar concepts and skills in courses at staff, senior staff, and management levels. We are still completing this process, and we hope by next year to have parallel courses running at all levels, with the upper-level courses incorporating a managerial perspective. This consistency will ensure that managers and staff are familiar with the same terminology, methodologies, and guidance. We also plan to increase the amount of training that we deliver to intact work groups and reduce the number of open enrollment classes. We believe that training the members of work groups together makes it more likely that the concepts taught in class will be reinforced and used on the job. Work unit–based training is also expected to have a direct effect on improving teamwork and intra-unit communication—important goals in an organization focused on quality. We plan to test these assumptions by conducting follow-up evaluations for selected courses.

Finally, in the spirit of quality management, we strive to assess the effectiveness of our training efforts continuously, and we revisit our delivery strategies. The challenges that the GAO faces change constantly, the needs of our work force change, and technological advances create new training demands.

References

Budget and Accounting Act of 1921. (P.L. 67–13, 42 Stat. 20, codified as amended at 31 U.S.C. 712).

Training Institute, U.S. General Accounting Office. *Training and Education: 1992–1993 Catalog.* Washington, D.C.: Training Institute, U.S. General Accounting Office, 1991.

NANCY KINGSBURY *is director for federal human resource management issues in the General Government Division of the U.S. General Accounting Office.*

TERRY E. HEDRICK *is director of the Training Institute at the U.S. General Accounting Office.*

*The procedures used to collect information for the Directory of
Evaluation Training Programs are described, and the results of the
survey are discussed. Tables list the programs identified in the
United States, Canada, and Australia.*

The 1994 Directory of Evaluation
Training Programs

*James W. Altschuld, Molly Engle, Carol Cullen,
Inyoung Kim, Barbara Rae Macce*

The American Evaluation Association (AEA) has periodically published a directory of evaluation training programs in the United States and Canada (May,
Fleischer, Schreier, and Cox, 1986; Conner, Clay, and Hill, 1980; Gephart and
Potter, 1976). May, Fleischer, Schreier, and Cox (1986) listed forty-six programs in six different types of settings. Programs located in education and psychology predominated. In late 1992, the board of the American Evaluation
Association commissioned a study to provide a current listing and description
of evaluation training programs. This chapter describes the study methodology, reports some of the study's findings, and tabulates the information about
evaluation training programs.

Methodology

Sample. Since 1986, numerous changes have occurred in the field of
evaluation that could affect the nature of training programs. Among them are
changes in the methods that evaluators use and improved understandings of
the relationship between evaluation and policy development. As a result, new
programs have emerged, others have changed or altered their content and
structure, and still others have ceased to exist.

The initial and perhaps most challenging task for the study team was to
develop a comprehensive sampling frame of potential candidates. We used the
following process to develop the sampling frame. First, we placed an
announcement in the call for papers for the AEA's 1992 annual conference.
The announcement asked AEA members to nominate candidates for the study.

The same announcement was posted in prominent locations at the 1992 conference site. By this means, we identified eighteen programs, including one in Australia. Second, we analyzed directory entries in Conner, Clay, and Hill (1980) and May, Fleischer, Schreier, and Cox (1986) to identify other potential candidates. Third, we collated the names collected at the AEA conference with the names culled from past directories and distributed the list to the AEA board for review and suggestions. By this procedure, we identified several more names. Fourth, we sent a letter to all members of the AEA's topical interest group on the teaching of evaluation (TIG-TOE). The letter described the directory study, defined what we meant by the term *program,* listed the candidates that we had already identified, and asked TIG-TOE members to review the list and identify other programs. By these means, we established a population of seventy-five likely programs, primarily from the United States.

Next, we examined the directory of the American Sociological Association for programs with evaluation content. We found twenty-two programs, which we contacted by telephone. This step allowed us to add two more names. Finally, in telephone conversations with the president of the Canadian Evaluation Society (CES) and CES regional presidents, we identified fifteen possible programs in Canada. The total sampling frame contained ninety-three elements: seventy-seven from the United States, fifteen from Canada, and one from Australia.

While it is possible that we omitted a few programs from the final mailing list, we are confident that the sampling frame was relatively complete. The fact that TIG-TOE members made very few additions corroborates this point.

Program Definition and Survey Design. To help respondents to determine whether their program should be documented in the directory, we provided the following working definition of *program*: A program consists of multiple courses, seminars, practicums, offerings, and so on designed to teach what the respondent considered to be evaluation principles and concepts. This statement made it possible to interpret *program* in a variety of ways, but it clearly excluded single-course "programs." We were not biased against single-course offerings. They have great value and importance for the field of evaluation, particularly in educating potential consumers of evaluation results and participants in the evaluation process, as the chapter by Morris in this sourcebook shows. However, single-course offerings serve different functions from those of the evaluation programs that we were seeking to identify for the directory.

We developed a six-page survey form that sought information on the following areas: program title; location and contact persons; degrees granted; year in which the program was started; the numbers of students admitted and graduated; placements of graduates; full-time teaching equivalents (FTEs) for the program; course descriptions; program goals; and areas of specialized content that are supportive of the program. We also included a series of questions related to research on evaluation training programs. We estimated that it would take between twenty-five and forty minutes to complete the survey form. We pilot tested the instrument and made some minor corrections.

Survey Administration. In late April 1993, we mailed surveys to U.S. respondents on a staggered basis, fifteen every three days, until the entire mailing to seventy-seven respondents was completed. Following established procedures for enhancing return rate (Altschuld and Lower, 1984; Altschuld and others, 1992), we called respondents shortly after we expected them to have received the survey. Later, we used follow-up postcards and additional phone calls to enhance the return and completion rates.

For the Canadian portion of the sample, we sent sets of survey materials (packaged and stamped for immediate mailing) to CES regional presidents for distribution to potential candidates. We called them several days after we expected the materials to have arrived to clarify details of the survey process. The regional presidents sent surveys to fifteen programs. If these programs had not responded within a few weeks, we mailed them follow-up reminders. We sent a survey to the Australian program in late April.

Survey Return Rate and Analysis Procedure. Ninety-three surveys were mailed. We received seventy-seven replies, for a response rate of 83 percent. Sixty-five of the United States candidates (84 percent) and twelve of the Australian and Canadian candidates (75 percent) returned completed surveys. From these seventy-seven responses, we identified forty-nine programs— thirty-eight in the United State and eleven in Australia and Canada. We added survey data to a database containing information from the earlier surveys that we had built with a commercial software package (Filemaker Pro 2, 1992). The software enabled us to calculate basic descriptive statistics across programs and to summarize program descriptions in tabular format.

Results

The number of programs identified—forty-nine—was only slightly higher than the tally for 1986, but the distribution of programs has changed: There are fewer programs in the United States (forty-four in 1986, thirty-eight now), and there are more programs in Australia and Canada (two in 1986, eleven now). We also identified three programs in government agencies and one nontraditional program that tailored training to the needs of students. These four programs did not exist in 1986. Slightly more than half of the programs— twenty-five of the forty-nine—have the identifier *evaluation* in their formal title. This finding is important as well as interesting, because it may represent limited evaluation visibility.

For the programs in universities in the United States, Australia, and Canada, the vast majority (76 percent) offer the Ph.D., the Ed.D., or both the doctoral and master's degrees. Another 14 percent of the programs offer the master's degree only, and the remaining 10 percent reported either that the evaluation courses were part of a degree obtained through another discipline or that the question was not applicable to their situation. The programs in the United States emphasized the doctoral degree somewhat more (84 percent) than the programs in Australia and Canada (45 percent).

The academic location of the programs that we identified underscores the changes that have occurred in evaluation training and the field of evaluation over the past few years. Of the forty-six programs identified in 1986, thirty-nine (85 percent) were in education, educational psychology, or psychology. That number had dropped to thirty-one (67 percent) in 1993. Thus, although evaluation training is still strongly aligned with education and psychology, the overall perspective of training has broadened to include other fields and government agencies.

Determining the size of programs is difficult. There are several indicators of size, and all are imprecise. The number of students admitted in one possible indicator. However, some programs have only a few students majoring in evaluation but large numbers of students enrolled in their courses. The number of faculty involved in a program is another possible indicator. Unfortunately, survey responses did not always distinguish between the number of faculty involved and the FTEs dedicated to evaluation training. The number of faculty shown in the directory tables is therefore a gross, not an exact, indicator of size.

The number of courses within a program is another imperfect indicator of size. Many respondents listed methodology courses and sequences (statistics, measurement, and so forth) as part of their evaluation program. Such courses may indeed be integral to some programs or contain what one respondent referred to as an infused evaluation content through the use of real-world, applied evaluation problems and examples. Others chose to view these courses and areas as being supportive of the program, not a direct part of it. Different and equally valid perspectives of what constitutes a program were apparent.

Despite the problems inherent in its use, we chose number of courses as the key variable for describing program size. By their sheer number, courses provide a general measure of the emphasis given to evaluation training. When reviewing the breakdown of size in the directory tables, readers should note that several programs sent extensive listings and even brochures about courses in statistics and measurement together with the completed survey form. Given the extensiveness of the list, we did not code these courses for entry into a directory table. Instead, the "Notes" column usually has a brief mention of the extensiveness of these offerings, and programs that supplied such lists were placed in the large-size-program category. Classifying programs by number of courses resulted in the following: There were fifteen (31 percent) small programs with two or three courses, thirteen (27 percent) medium programs with four to six courses, and twenty-one (43 percent) large programs with seven courses or more.

The findings about program goals in this most recent survey stress the practitioner orientation that Fitzpatrick advocates in her contribution to this sourcebook. Most programs emphasized training for the conduct of evaluations, for development of general understandings of the field, or for both. Contributing to evaluation research and teaching evaluation were much less prominent. Of the courses offered, statistics (15 percent), methodology (14 percent), practicums (11 percent), introductory courses (11 percent), and measurement (10 percent) were most often cited, followed by seminars (6 percent) and qualitative methods (5 percent).

The placement of graduates follows the trends suggested by the preceding data. In 1986, 23 percent of the graduates were placed in academic faculty positions. In 1993, approximately 17 percent of the graduates were placed in universities and another 9 percent in research centers. (The research centers may be associated with academic institutions, and they probably include both basic research and applied endeavors.) Twenty-four percent of the placements were in federal, state, or local government. The other major settings for placement were private consulting (15 percent), nonprofit agencies (13 percent), and business and industry (12 percent). Education still remains the primary field for employment (30 percent), although the figures indicate a 7 percent drop from 1986. This decrease was to be anticipated given the decrease in training programs located in education departments. Human services was the next most often occurring field (17 percent versus 13 percent in 1986). All other possible fields were represented by 10 percent or less of the placements. A combined 32 percent of the responses were of the *data not available, highly varied,* or *other* variety.

Discussion

Although more data collected over a longer period of time would be helpful for understanding placement, we can note several trends in the data. There has been some shift away from academic placements (possibly due to budgetary pressures) and education settings toward more diverse ones. This finding and the fact that 53 percent of all programs included practicums, internships, fieldwork, or related activities suggest that the focus may be shifting from evaluator as researcher to evaluator as practitioner.

Data about problems encountered in the development of evaluation programs, the use of evaluation standards, potential developments in the future, and other aspects of evaluation programs were also collected during the survey process, but we will not report them here. So we can portray a broad description of programs, we will reserve comparisons between large and small programs and between programs in education and programs in psychology or other fields for presentation elsewhere.

We did note during the course of the study that several programs that were no longer in existence may have been maintained exclusively by one or two key faculty. If those individuals left or retired, continuation of the program was no longer possible. In some cases, smaller programs may have been dropped in the absence of stable and enduring resources.

We wholeheartedly encourage others to engage in research on evaluation training. Here are some of the questions that could be asked: How do graduates view the value of their training? What changes in evaluation training programs would they recommend? What functions should the AEA serve in regard to evaluation training programs? Are there evaluation training programs in Europe, Asia, South America, and Africa? What are they like?

These are just some of the questions that can be asked about training. Providing programs for the training of professional evaluators is essential for the survival and development of the field. The study of professional preparation should have long-term dividends for the training and practice of evaluators.

The Directory Tables and How to Use Them

Table 7.1 (on pp. 78–89) is the 1994 directory for programs in the United States. Table 7.2 (on pp. 90–93) presents information about the programs in Australia and Canada. The tables should be easy to understand, and the codes that have been used are relatively self-explanatory. Column one lists the institution or agency in which the program is located (colleges and departments) and gives its address. Column two has the formal title (if applicable) and name of the key contact person or persons. Column three shows the degrees offered and the year in which the program was started. Column four gives the total number of faculty involved in the program (not necessarily the same as FTEs) and the program goals. Program goals are indicated by codes corresponding to the underlined portions of the following words:

Conduct Evaluations, Develop General Understandings, Contribute to Evaluation Research, and Teach Evaluation.)

Column five contains information about courses and offerings. It uses the following codes for this information: Introduction = introductory courses; Methodology = courses dealing with descriptions and explanations of methods; Design = courses emphasizing experimental, quasi-experimental, or evaluation design; Measurement = instruction in measurement, scaling, and/or instrumentation; and Practicum = practicums, apprenticeships, fieldwork, internships, and/or independent study. Statistics, Performance Appraisal, Qualitative Methods, Needs Assessment, Cost-Benefit Analysis, and Seminar are self-explanatory. Other means that the courses did not fit any of the other codes. The number in parentheses beside a course code indicates the number of such courses or offerings provided by the program. If a course combined features of categories, we counted it under each category.

Column six contains information about employment placement. We used the following codes for placement settings: Federal Government, Government (local and state governments), B&I (business and industry), T&D (training and development), Health, and Mental Health. Because some programs provided data on actual numbers of placements and others did not, the number of individuals placed is not available. Column seven contains brief descriptions of any special features of the program and of the courses described as Other. The abbreviations used in this column—for example, *eval., stat., edu.*—should be easy to understand.

The reader should keep two things in mind when reviewing the directory tables. First, as already noted, the size of a program cannot be inferred from the number of faculty involved. Second, the information about courses and offerings is indicative, not definitive, of program content. Some respondents perceived their program as consisting of courses that did not include statistics, measurement, or other related areas. Instead, they viewed these courses as supportive of the evaluation emphasis and therefore limited their descriptions to the topics that they associated with their definition of *evaluation program*. Other respondents, taking a more inclusive perspective, placed such courses in their descriptions. It is quite possible that, through the use of evaluation settings and problems, courses in statistics, measurement, and instrument development may have a very strong, infused evaluation component.

The understanding of the expression *evaluation program* that guided development of the survey instrument gave respondents a great deal of latitude in depicting their program. We believe that other studies will be necessary if we are to understand fully what the dimensions of evaluation curricula are or should be. We urge users of the directory tables to communicate with the contacts that they identify for detailed information about individual programs.

References

Altschuld, J. W., Thomas, P. M., McColskey, W. H., Smith, D. H., Wiesmann, W. W., and Lower, M. A. "Mailed Evaluation Questionnaires: Replications of a 96 Percent Return Rate Procedure." *Evaluation and Program Planning*, 1992, *15*, 21–28.

Altschuld, J. W., and Lower, M. A. "Improving Mailed Questionnaires: Analysis of a 96 Percent Return Rate." In D. C. Lockhart (ed.), *Making Effective Use of Mailed Questionnaires*. New Directions for Program Evaluation, no. 21. San Francisco: Jossey-Bass, 1984.

Conner, R. F., Clay, T., and Hill, P. *Directory of Evaluation Training*. Washington, D.C.: Pintail Press, 1980.

FileMaker Pro 2. Claris Corporation, 1992.

Gephart, W. J., and Potter, W. J. *Evaluation Training Catalog*. Bloomington, Ind.: Phi Delta Kappa, 1976.

May, R. M., Fleischer, M., Sheirer, C. J., and Cox, G. B. "Directory of Evaluation Training Programs." In B. G. Davis (ed.), *Teaching of Evaluation Across the Disciplines*. New Directions for Program Evaluation, no. 29. San Francisco: Jossey-Bass, 1986.

Table 7.1. Evaluation Training Programs in the United States

Institution and Department	Program Title and Contact(s)	Degree(s) and Year Program Began	Number of Faculty Involved and Program Goal(s)	
American University School of Public Affairs Department of Public Administration 4400 Massachusetts Avenue N.W. Washington, DC 20016	Master in Public Administration (MPA) Laura I. Langbein (202) 885-6233 langbei@american.edu	Master's 1985	2	Conduct Eval Develop Gen Unstds
Ball State University Teacher's College Educational Leadership Muncie, IN 47306	Evaluation and Staff Development James H. McElhinney (317) 285-5348	Part of other graduate programs 1968	2	Conduct Eval Develop Gen Unstds
Columbia University Teacher's College Department of Measurement, Evaluation, & Statistics 525 W. 120 Street New York, NY 10027	Measurement & Evaluation Richard M. Wolf (212) 678-3355 rmwolf@cutcv2	Ph.D. Master's 1968	5	Conduct Eval Develop Gen Unstds
Cornell University College of Human Ecology Department of Human Service Studies N132 MVR Hall Ithaca, NY 14853	Program Evaluation & Planning William Trochim Jennifer Greene (607) 255-2506	Ph.D. Master's 1980	2.5	Conduct Eval Develop Gen Unstds Contribute to Eval Rsch Teach Eval
Florida State University Department of Educational Research 307 F. Stone Building Tallahassee, FL 32306	Program Evaluation Track Garrett R. Foster J. G. Beard (904) 644-8794	Ph.D. Master's Specialist Certification 1968	7	Conduct Eval Develop Gen Unstds Contribute to Eval Rsch Teach Eval
General Accounting Office Training Institute Evaluator Curriculum 441 G Street, N.W. Room 7822 Washington, DC 20548	Evaluator Curriculum Anne Klein, Terry E. Hedrick (202) 512-8674	Not applicable 1989	3	Conduct Eval
Hofstra University College of Liberal Arts & Sciences Department of Psychology Hempstead, NY 11550	Industrial & Organizational Psychology (IO) William Metlay (516)292-6168	Master's 1993	11	Conduct Eval Develop Gen Unstds

| Courses/ Offerings | Placement | | Notes |
	Setting(s)	Field(s)	
Meth (1), Policy (2)	Fed Govt Govt (Local) Consul	Varied	Two stat. courses are prerequisites for the methods course.
Intro & Pract (1), PA (1), Pract (1), Seminar (1)	Univ Fed Govt Research Ctr Nonprofit B&I Consul	Hum Serv Edu T&D Other	Doctoral students often do eval. research for dissertations.
Intro & Meth (2)	Univ Research Ctr B&I	Edu	Other courses in meas. and stat. as related to technical competence.
Intro (1), Meth (1), Des (1), Meas (1), Pract (2), Qual (1), Seminar (2)	Not available	Not available	Other methods courses on campus for depth and topically focused planning and policy courses are also available. Program is for eval. researchers.
Intro (1), Meth (1), Des (1), Meas (2), Stat (3), Qual (3), PA (1), Pract (1), NA (1), Other (3)	Univ Govt (State) Research Ctr Nonprofit B&I Consul Public School Other	Hum Serv Edu Hlth Agr T&D Policy Other	Other courses include economic eval, eval. of training, dissertation research, and a minor in the students area of interest.
Program consists of an extensive set of short courses. In addition to the 3 faculty, up to 120 more are involved in instruction.	Fed Govt	Varied (across many Fed Govt fields)	See the Chapter by Kingsbury and Hedrick in this volume for a description of the program.
Evaluation content is heavily imbedded in numerous IO courses.	Not available	Not available	None

Table 7.1. *(continued)*

Institution and Department	Program Title and Contact(s)	Degree(s) and Year Program Began	Number of Faculty Involved and Program Goal(s)
Indiana University Department of Counseling & Educational Psychology Wright Education 201 N. Rose Avenue Bloomington, IN 47405	Inquiry Methodology Thomas Schwandt (812) 856-8341	Ph.D. 1980	8 Conduct Eval Develop Gen Unstds Contribute to Eval Rsch Teach Eval
Iowa State University College of Agriculture Agricultural Education & Studies 217 Curtis Hall Ames, IA 50011	Not applicable Julia A. Gamon (515) 294-0897	Not applicable 1979	1 Conduct Eval Develop Gen Unstds Contribute to Eval Rsch Teach Eval
Iowa State University College of Education Professional Studies in Education Ames, IA 50011	Research & Evaluation Mary E. Huba (515) 294-7358 eimeh@isuvax	Ph.D. Master's 1975	5 Conduct Eval Develop Gen Unstds Contribute to Eval Rsch
Lehigh University Center for Social Research 516 Brodhead Avenue Bethlehem, PA 18015	Ph.D. Program in Applied Social Research Donald T. Campbell, Diane T. Hyland (215) 758-4528 dtc0@lehigh.edu	Ph.D. 1986	4 Conduct Eval Develop Gen Unstds Contribute to Eval Rsch
Memphis State University College of Arts and Sciences Department of Psychology Memphis, TN 38152	Research Design & Statistics William R. Shadish (901) 678-4687 shadishwr@msuvx1. memst.edu	Ph.D. 1993	6 Conduct Eval Develop Gen Unstds (methods)
Michigan State University Department of Psychology Graduate Program 129 PYR East Lansing, MI 48824-1117	Ecological/Community Psychology, Graduate Program William S. Davidson, II (517) 353-5015 wsd@psy.ssc.banyon. msu.edu	Ph.D. 1969	5 Conduct Eval Develop Gen Unstds
Ohio State University College of Education Educational Services & Research 1945 North High Street 287 Arps Hall Columbus, OH 43210-1172	Educational Research & Evaluation James W. Altschuld Donald L. Haefele (614) 292-3239 jaltschu@magnus.acs. ohio-state.edu Applied Experimental	Ph.D. Master's 1982	2 Conduct Eval Develop Gen Unstds Contribute to Eval Rsch Teach Eval

Courses/ Offerings	Placement		Notes
	Setting(s)	Field(s)	
Intro (1), Meth (1), Meas (1), Qual (1), Pract (1)	Not available	Not available	Other ralated courses include stat, (3), social and political philosophy (1), ed. policy studies (1), organizational theory and behavior (varied).
Intro (1), Other (1)	Govt	Edu	The other eval. course is in regard to program development and eval. in agricultural extension edu. Internships and special projects in eval. are also available.
Intro (1), Pract (1), Seminar (1)	Univ Govt Nonprofit B&I Consul Other	Edu Hlth Other	Numerous courses in such areas as stat., research design, computer data analysis, meas., and qual. research methods are available in Research & Eval. Section, other sections, and other departments.
See Notes	Varied	Varied	Very extensive program in stat., design, and research methods. Program includes courses related to policy, qualitative methods, design applied to evaluation problems, and other related areas.
Intro (1), Des (1), Meas (1), Stat(4)	Not applicable	Not applicable	Courses in eval. are also offered in political science and education.
Intro (2), Meth (1), Pract (1), Seminar (numerous)	Univ Fed Govt Govt Nonprofit	Not available	All courses are in community psychology.
Intro (1), Meth (1), PA (2), NA (2), Pract (1)	Univ Consul Research Ctr Other	Edu	Majors in eval are required to take stat. and meas. as well as have a specialized cognate area (usually in education).

Table 7.1. (continued)

Institution and Department	Program Title and Contact(s)	Degree(s) and Year Program Began	Number of Faculty Involved and Program Goal(s)	
Southern Illinois University Department of Psychology Carbondale, IL 62901	Psychology Jack McKillip (618) 536-2301	Ph.D. 1978	6	Conduct Eval Develop Gen Unstds
Syracuse University School of Education Department of Instructional Design, Develop. & Eval. (IDD&E) 330 Huntington Hall Syracuse, NY 13244-2340	Evaluation training is one emphasis within the large program (IDD&E) Nick L. Smith (315) 443-3704 nismith@suvm	Ph.D. Ed.D. Master's Certification 1947 (total prog)	3 or 4	Conduct Eval Develop Gen Unstds Contribute to Eval Rsch Teach Eval
Temple University Educational Psychology RA 217, TU-004-00 Philadelphia, PA 19122	Psychological Studies in Education Glenn E. Snelbecker (215) 204-6109	Ph.D. Master's Date not available	1	Conduct Eval Develop Gen Unstds
Union Institute Graduate School 440 East McMillian Street Cincinnati, OH 45206	Evaluation and Organizational Development Michael Quinn Patton (513) 861-6400 800-486-3116	Ph.D. 1987	8	Purpose depends on individual student needs and interests.
University of Alabama College of Education Area of Prefessional Studies P.O. Box 870231 Tuscaloosa, AL 35487-0231	Program in Educational Research Brad Chissom (205) 348-1186	Ph.D. Specialist 1976	5	Conduct Eval Develop Gen Unstds Contribute to Eval Rsch
University of Albany, SUNY School of Education Education Theory & Practice 1400 Washington Avenue Albany, NY 12222	Program Evaluation Specialization Dianna L. Newman, Sandra Mathison, David Chapman (518) 442-5018	Ed.D. Master's Certification 1985	3	Conduct Eval Develop Gen Unstds Contribute to Eval Rsch
University of Arizona Department of Psychology Tucson, AZ 85721	Methodology and Program Evaluation Lee Sechrest (603) 621-9182 secrest@arizvms	Ph.D. 1988	6	Conduct Eval Develop Gen Unstds

Courses/ Offerings	Placement		Notes
	Setting(s)	Field(s)	
Intro (1), Des (1), Meas (1), Stat (Numerous), NA (1), Pract (1), Other (2)	Nonprofit B&I Consul	Edu T&D Others	Other courses include decision theory and the meas. of change. Students take stat. and courses in community psychology intervention and organizational change and development.
Meth (2), C-BA (1), Other (1)	Varied	Varied	The other course deals with eval. theory. Eval. topics are also taught in courses on IDD & E. Several research methods course are required of all doctoral students. Many applied evaluation experiences are available.
Intro (1), Des (1), Pract (2)	Not available	Not available	Not a formal program but students can develop an eval. emphasis through a variety of meas. and stat. courses and 1–2 semesters of an eval. apprenticeship.
Interdisciplinary, accredited, nontraditional, individually designed & mentored program	See Notes	See Notes	Program is nonresidential, learner centered, and flexible. Setting(s) and field(s) are often determined by current setting and learner's field.
Intro (1), Meth (1), Des (1), Meas (5), Stat (5), Qual (1), Pract (2), Seminar (1), Other (1)	Not available	Not available	The other course focuses on readings in eval. Dissertation research is also part of the program.
Doctoral Level: Intro (1), Meth (2), Seminar (3), Pract (2), Other (1) Master's Level: Intro (1), Meas (3), Pract (1), Other (1)	Univ Govt Research Ctr B&I Consul	Hum Serv Edu Hlth Mhlth	The doctoral level includes a course on international eval., and the master's level includes a course on the eval. of educational material. Eval. of personnel and eval. ethics courses are also available in ed. admin.
Meth & Des (2), Meas (1), Stat (Numerous)	Not available	Not available	None

Table 7.1. *(continued)*

Institution and Department	Program Title and Contact(s)	Degree(s) and Year Program Began	Number of Faculty Involved and Program Goal(s)	
University of California, Berkeley Graduate School of Education Educational Administration Berkeley, CA 94720	Not applicable James C. Stone (510) 642-0709	Ph.D. Ed.D. Date not applicable	1	Develop Gen Unstds
University of California, Berkeley School of Public Health 416 Warren Hall Berkeley, CA 94720	Health Policy and Administration Thomas G. Rundall (510) 642-4606	Dr. P.H. Ph.D. Master's 1980	7	Develop Gen Unstds
University of California, Irvine School of Social Ecology Irvine, CA 92717	Not applicable Ross Conner, Kay Helwig (714) 856-6746 rfconner@ucf.edu	Ph.D. Date not available	10	See Notes
University of Chicago Department of Education 5835 S. Kimbark Street Chicago, IL 60637-1609	Measurement, Evaluation & Statistical Analysis Susan Stodolsky (312) 702-1599 stdsue@paideia.spc. uchicago.edu	Ph.D. Master's 1963	4	Conduct Eval Develop Gen Unstds Contribute to Eval Rsch Teach Eval
University of Maryland College of Education Measurement, Statistics & Evaluation College Park, MD 20742	Measurement, Statistics & Evaluation Robert W. Lissitz (301) 405-3620 rl27@umail.umd.edu	PhD. Master's 1970	15	Conduct Eval Develop Gen Unstds Contribute to Eval Rsch Teach Eval
University of Minnesota Department of Educational Psychology 210 Burton Hall Minneapolis, MN 55455	Not applicable Wayne W. Welch (612) 624-4095 wwelch@vx.cis.umn.edu	Ph.D. Master's 1971	3	Conduct Eval Develop Gen Unstds Contribute to Eval Rsch
University of Nebraska Teachers College Department of Educational Psychology 116 Bancroft Lincoln, NE 68512	Quantitative & Qualitative Methods in Education (QQM in E) Barbara Plake (402) 472-3280	Ph.D. Master's 1985 for QQM in E.	18	Conduct Eval Develop Gen Unstds

Courses/ Offerings	Placement Setting(s)	Field(s)	Notes
Meth (1), Qual (1), Stat (2)	Not available	Not available	None
Intro (1), Meth (3), Meas (2), Stat (1), Qual (1), Pract (1), Other (1)	Not available	Not available	The other course is an advanced course in health program eval. Students also take epidemiology and biostatistics.
Intro (1), Des (1), Meth (1), Stat (5), Other (2)	Univ Fed Govt Govt Research Ctr Nonprofit B&I Consul	Human Serv Criminal Justice Policy Social Sci. Other	Goal of program is to create understandings of eval. in relation to environmental analysis, criminology, law and society, health psychology, urban and regional planning, psychology and social behavior. Other courses are related to specialized area of student emphasis.
Intro (1), Meas (3), Stat (2), Des & Seminar (1), Other (3)	Univ Govt Nonprofit B&I Consul Other	Edu Mhlth T&D Other	The other courses are analysis of classroom activity, eval. data analysis, eval. data analysis, and eval workshop. Some students work at Board of Ed., Center for School Improvement and Consortium on Chicago School Reform. Students also develop personal portfolios.
Intro (1), Des (1), Meas (3), Pract (1), Seminar (1), Meth (1), Stat (8), Other (1)	Univ Fed Govt Nonprofit Consul	Hum Serv Edu T&D Policy	Special topics in stat. are also offered.
Intro & Meth (1), Meas (1), Pract (1), Seminar (1), Other (1)	Univ Govt	Hum Serv Edu	A problems in eval. course in also offered.
Intro (1), Pract (1)	Not available	Not available	Educational stat., meas, and research methods courses provide students with fundamental skills needed to conduct evals. Eval. courses are part of QQM in E program.

Table 7.1. *(continued)*

Institution and Department	Program Title and Contact(s)	Degree(s) and Year Program Began	Number of Faculty Involved and Program Goal(s)	
University of North Carolina Psychology/Quantitative Program CB #3270, Davie Hall Chapel Hill, NC 27599-3270	Quantitative Methods in Evaluation David Thissen (919) 962-5036 dthissen@uncvm1.oit.un c.edu	Ph.D. 1952	11	Conduct Eval Develop Gen Unstds
University of North Carolina School of Education Educational Research Methodology Curry Building Greensboro, NC 27412-5001	Educational Research Methodology John C. Busch, Rita G. O'Sullivan (919) 334-5100	Ph.D. Master's 1976 (Master's) 1985 (Doctoral)	5	Conduct Eval Develop Gen Unstds Contribute to Eval Rsch Teach Eval
University of Northern Colorado College of Education Educational Psychology, Research & Evaluation Greeley, CO 80639	Educational Psychology, Research & Evaluation Coordinator (303) 351-2807	Ph.D. Master's Before 1980	6	Conduct Eval Develop Gen Unstds
University of Pittsburgh Department of Administrative & Policy Studies 5501 Forbes Quadrangle Pittsburgh, PA 15260	Policy, Planning & Evaluation Program R. Tony Eichelberger, William Cooley (412) 624-7093	Ed.D. Master's 1985	15	Conduct Eval Develop Gen Unstds
University of Pittsburgh School of Social Work 2112 Cathedral of Learning Pittsburgh, PA 15260	Not applicable Michael A. Patchner (412) 624-6345	Ph.D. 1945 DSW 1963 Ph.D.	9	Conduct Eval Develop Gen Unstds Contribute to Eval Rsch Teach Eval
University of Texas, El Paso Department of Sociology El Paso, TX 79968-0558	Evaluation Planning-Training Program Howard C. Daudistel (915) 747-5740 ckcutep.bitnet	Master's 1974	3	Conduct Eval Develop Gen Unstds

Courses/ Offerings	Placement		Notes
	Setting(s)	Field(s)	
Intro (1), Meth (2), Other (numerous)	Fed Govt Govt B&I Consul	Hum Serv Edu Hlth T&D Soc Sci	An extensive set of stat. and meas. courses is also offered as part of the program.
Intro (1), Meth (1), Seminar (1), Pract (1)	Univ Govt Other	Edu Other	Students also take stat., meas., qualitative methods, and survey research classes.
Intro (1), Meth (3), Meas (2), Stat (3), Qual (1), Pract (numerous)	Univ B&I Other	Edu	The department of mathematics and applied stat. offers many support courses for the program.
Intro (1), Meth (3), Pract (1), Seminar (1), Other (6)	Univ Fed Govt Govt Research Ctr Nonprofit B&I Consul	Hum Serv Edu Hlth Mhlth Policy Other	Other eval. courses are international eval., eval. and decision making, eval. and program planning, systems design for res., and prog. planning (2). Numerous disciplined inquiry core courses are required. Planning and policy courses in social work or the graduate school of public and international affairs are available.
Meth (3), Stat (2), Qual (1)	Univ Govt Nonprofit	Hum Serv	Related courses include social policy analysis (2) and electives from the school of social work as well as those within the university. One of the methods courses in program is focused on evaluating communities.
See Notes	Not available	Not available	Program is currently not in place, but a redesigned program is being planned and will be operational in 1994–1995.

Table 7.1. *(continued)*

Institution and Department	Program Title and Contact(s)	Degree(s) and Year Program Began	Number of Faculty Involved and Program Goal(s)	
University of Virginia School of Education Department of Educational Studies 405 Emmet Street Charlottesville, VA 22903	Program in Educational Evaluation Michael S. Caldwell, Robert W. Covert, Mary Ellwein (804) 924-7341 rwc3q@virginia.edu	Ph.D. Ed.D. Master's 1970	3	Not available
Utah State University Department of Psychology UMC 2810 Logan, UT 84322-2810	Research and Evaluation Methodology Blaine R. Worthen (801)750-1447	Ph.D. 1985	9	Conduct Eval Develop Gen Unstds Contribute to Eval Rsch Teach Eval
Vanderbilt University Peabody College Department of Human Resources Box 90 GPC Nashville, TN 37203	Graduate Program in Policy Development & Program Eval (PDPE) Mark W. Lipsey (615) 343-1586	Ph.D. Master's 1983	21	Conduct Eval Develop Gen Unstds
Western Michigan University Department of Educational Leadership Kalamazoo, MI 49008-5178	Evaluation, Measurement and Research Design James R. Sanders (616) 387-5895 james. sanders@ wmich.edu	Ph.D. Ed.D. Master's 1973	6	Conduct Eval Develop Gen Unstds Contribute to Eval Rsch Teach Eval

Source: Copyright 1994, American Evaluation Association; reprinted with permission.

Courses/	Placement		Notes
Offerings	Setting(s)	Field(s)	
Intro (1), Des (1), Meas (1), Qual (2), Pract (1), Other (1)	Univ Govt Research Ctr Nonprofit B&I Consul Other	Hum Serv Edu Mhlth	The program includes a multicultural education course as the other course. All students take a minimum of four research courses in such areas as stat. and computer applications.
Intro (1), Meth (5), Pract (3), Stat (5), Des (2), Qual (1), Meas (4), Other (3) Seminar (2)	Univ Research Ctr	Edu Soc Sci	Other courses include grant writing, philosophy of science, and computer program usage. Program is dependent on achieving certain competencies via mentored, hands-on analyzing, presenting, and publishing activities.
Intro (1), Meth (1), Seminar (2), Other (1)	Univ Fed Govt Govt Nonprofit B&I Consul Other	Edu Hlth Justice Mhlth	The other course is focused on political and organizational analysis. Additional related courses include economics and ethics.
Intro (1), PA (1), Pract (2), Seminar (1), Other (1)	Univ Nonprofit B&I School district	Edu	The other course relates to dissertation research. Students also take a research sequence, a meas. sequence, and a related cognate area, such as computer applications, stat., or policy analysis.

Table 7.2. Evaluation Training Programs in the Australia and Canada

Institution and Department	Program Title and Contact(s)	Degree(s) and Year Program Began	Number of Faculty Involved and Program Goal(s)	
Australia				
The University of Melbourne Institute of Education Department of Policy, Context, & Evaluation Studies Parkville, Victoria Australia 3052	Master of Evaluation/ Post-Graduate Diploma in Evaluation John M. Owen (03) 344-8394 john.owen@muwayf. unimelb.edu.au	Master's Postgrad. Diploma 1982	4	Conduct Eval
Canada				
Deputy Comptroller General Evaluation and Audit Branch 10th Floor, West Tower 300 Laurier Avenue, W. Ottawa, Ontario Canada, K1A 1E4	Not applicable Doug Wood (613) 992-9160	Not applicable Not available	–	Conduct Eval Develop Gen Unstds
Ecole Nationale d'Administration Publique Evaluation of Public Programs 945 Wolfe Sainte-Foy, Quebec Canada, G1V 3J6	Evaluation of Public Programs Maurice Patry (418) 657-2485	Master's 1991	15	Conduct Eval Contribute to Eval Rsch
University of Calgary Educational Policy & Administrative Studies 940 Ed. Tower Calgary, Alberta Canada, T2N 1N4	Policy Studies Specialization Alice Boberg, R. O'Reilly (403) 220-5675	Ph.D. Master's 1981	5	Conduct Eval Develop Gen Unstds Contribute to Eval Rsch
University of Guelph Department of Psychology Guelph, Ontario Canada, N1G 2W1	Applied Social Psychology Karen Korabik (519) 824-4120 psykaren@vm. voguelph.ca	Ph.D. 1978	6	Conduct Eval
University of Lethbridge 4401 University Drive Lethbridge, Alberta Canada, T1K 3M4	Not applicable Myrna Greene (403) 329-2251	Not applicable Not applicable	1	Develop Gen Unstds

| Courses/ Offerings | Placement | | Notes |
	Setting(s)	Field(s)	
Intro (1), Stat (1), Qual (1), Pract (1), Other (3)	Not available	Not available	The other courses include eval. of large scale programs, eval. theory, and knowledge utilization and change.
See Notes	Not applicable	Not applicable	A series of four workshops with up to seventeen full days of training is available in auditing, eval., eval. methods, assessing service quality and program performance.
Intro (1), Stat (1), Policy (1), C-BA (1), Pract (1), Seminar (1)	Not available	Not available	A large number of other courses are also available through ENAP.
Intro & Des (1), Stat (1), Qual (1), Policy (1), Other (1)	Consul Other	Edu	The other course focuses on survey research. A number of courses in the program are seen as supportive of the intro. and design course.
Des & NA (1), Meth (1), Pract (numerous)	Nonprofit Consul	Hum Serv Edu	None
Intro (1), Other (2)	Not available	Not available	Not a formal program, but courses are offered as staff is available. The two other courses are curriculum eval. and the eval. of student learning.

Table 7.2. *(continued)*

Institution and Department	Program Title and Contact(s)	Degree(s) and Year Program Began	Number of Faculty Involved and Program Goal(s)	
University of Manitoba Faculty of Management Business Administration Winnipeg, Manitoba Canada, R3T 2N2	Not applicable Norm Frohlich (204) 474-6385 frohlic@ccm. umanitoba.ca	Master's 1979	1	Conduct Eval
University of Saskatchewan College of Education Curriculum Studies Saskatoon, SK Canada, S7N 0W0	College of Education Alan Ryan (306) 966-7574	Ph.D. Ed.D. 1985	3	Conduct Eval Develop Gen Unstds
University of Victoria Faculty of Human & Social Development School of Public Administration Victoria, British Columbia Canada	Public Administration, with a concentration in Evaluation & Policy Analysis James McDavid (604) 721-8050 mconnoll@uvvm. uvic.ca	Master's 1974	15	Conduct Eval Develop Gen Unstds
University of Waterloo Department of Health Studies & Gerontology Waterloo, Ontario Canada, N2L 3G1	Multidisciplinary Dept. (Psychology, Epidemiology, Biochemistry) Anita Myers (519) 885-1211	Ph.D. Master's 1978	12	Conduct Eval Develop Gen Unstds
University of Windsor Department of Psychology 401 Sunset Avenue Windsor, Ontario Canada, N9B 3P4	Program Evaluation Durhane Wong-Rieger (519) 253-4232	Ph.D. 1983	8	Conduct Eval Develop Gen Unstds

Source: Copyright 1994, American Evaluation Association; reprinted with permission.

Courses/	Placement		Notes
Offerings	Setting(s)	Field(s)	
Meth (1), Policy (1)	Not available	Not available	The methods course deals with eval. techniques for management. Other supportive courses include accounting, finance, economics, and stat. The two program courses train individuals to be intelligent consumers of eval.
Intro & Meth (1), Pract (1)	Univ	Edu	Supportive courses include general curriculum in research methods and test construction in educational psychology.
Meth (3), Policy (1), C-BA (1)	Fed Govt Govt Nonprofit Consul Other	Hum Serv Edu Other	There are core methodology courses (3) in administration and courses in economics that support the program.
Intro & Pract (1), C-BA & Strategic Planning (1), Other (1)	Univ Fed Govt Govt Research Ctr Nonprofit Consul	Hum Serv Edu Mhlth	The other course relates to program development and service delivery for the elderly. The honors program includes community health, models of health behavior, epidemiology, methods, and stat. Strong methodology base is seen as important for eval. courses.
Intro (1), Meth (1), Pract (2)	Fed Govt Research Ctr. B&I Consul	Not available	Related course work in research methods consultation, and organizational development.

JAMES W. ALTSCHULD is associate professor in educational research and evaluation and evaluation coordinator for the National Center for Science Teaching and Learning at The Ohio State University.

MOLLY ENGLE is assistant professor in the School of Medicine at the University of Alabama at Birmingham.

CAROL CULLEN is an instructor in educational research and evaluation at The Ohio State University and a private consultant in Delaware, Ohio.

INYOUNG KIM is a doctoral candidate in educational research and evaluation at The Ohio State University.

BARBARA RAE MACCE is research and development officer for the National Center for Science Teaching and Learning at The Ohio State University.

INDEX

Ordering Information

New Directions for Program Evaluation is a series of paperback books that presents the latest techniques and procedures for conducting useful evaluation studies of all types of programs. Books in the series are published quarterly in Spring, Summer, Fall, and Winter and are available for purchase by subscription as well as by single copy.

Subscriptions for 1994 cost $54.00 for individuals (a savings of 34 percent over single-copy prices) and $75.00 for institutions, agencies, and libraries. Please do not send institutional checks for personal subscriptions. Standing orders are accepted.

Single copies cost $17.95 when payment accompanies order. (California, New Jersey, New York, and Washington, D.C., residents please include appropriate sales tax.) Billed orders will be charged postage and handling.

Discounts for quantity orders are available. Please write to the address below for information.

All orders must include either the name of an individual or an official purchase order number. Please submit your order as follows:
   Subscriptions: specify series and year subscription is to begin
   Single copies: include individual title code (such as PE59)

Mail all orders to:
   Jossey-Bass Publishers
   350 Sansome Street
   San Francisco, California 94104-1342

For subscription sales outside of the United States, contact:
   any international subscription agency or Jossey-Bass directly.